OPEN YOUR HEART

with *Singing*

"I love your book very much. Whenever I want to change a sad mood, for instance, I read a few pages and immediately feel much better."

—Monika Spoeck, Astrologer,
Vienna, Austria

"The ability to open one's heart mindfully and trust in life's experiences can be quite a balancing act. Jules Kennedy's book shows us a way to achieve this balance, through the immediacy of song and music, and through highly effective visualization techniques that take the reader's journey to deeper levels of understanding. I thoroughly recommend this author."

—Amrieka Takhar, Social Entrepreneur and Founder/
Director of Mieka Designs, New Delhi, India
miekadesigns.com

OPEN YOUR HEART
with *Singing*

Mastering Life through Love of Song

JULES KENNEDY

DreamTime Publishing, Inc.

DreamTime Publishing, Inc., books are available at special quantity discounts for bulk purchases for sales promotions, premiums, fund-raising, and educational needs. Please contact us at www.DreamTimePublishing.com for additional information.

Library of Congress Cataloging-in-Publication Data
Kennedy, Jules.
    Open your heart with singing : mastering life through love of song / Jules Kennedy. — 1st ed.
        p. cm.
    ISBN 978-1-60166-007-7 (trade pbk.)
    1. Music—Psychological aspects. 2. Singing—Psychological aspects. 3. Meditation—Therapeutic use. 4. Stress—Psychological therapy. I. Title.

    ML3920.K37   2007
    783'.011—dc22

                                                        2007007422

Branding, website, and cover design for DreamTime Publishing by
    Rearden Killion • www.reardenkillion.com
Illustrations by Janice Marie Phelps • www.janicephelps.com
Text layout and design by Gary A. Rosenberg • www.garyarosenberg.com

This publication is designed to provide accurate and authoritative information in regard to the subject matter covered. It is sold with the understanding that the publisher is not engaged in rendering legal, accounting, or other professional service. If legal advice or other expert assistance is required, the services of a competent professional person should be sought.
    —*From a declaration of principles jointly adopted by a committee of the American Bar Association and a committee of publishers.*

This book is printed on recycled, acid-free paper containing a minimum of 50% recycled, de-inked fiber.

3 3988 10070 0001

Contents

Note from the Publisher

Balancing the overall mission of a series of books with each author's individual creativity and vision is an enjoyable and rewarding challenge. The goal of this note is to tie the loose ends together to make your experience with this book as meaningful as possible.

We have two goals with the Open Your Heart series. One is to provide you with practical advice about your hobby or interest, in this case singing. We trust this advice will increase your ongoing enjoyment of song, or perhaps even encourage you to rediscover your love of singing.

Our second goal is to help you use what you know and love to make the rest of your life happier and easier. This process worked in different ways for each of our writers, so it will likely work in different ways for each of you. For some, it's a matter of becoming more self-aware. Just realizing what makes you happy when you sing, and then gradually learning to use those feelings as a barometer when dealing with your job, relationships, and other issues could be an important first step. For others, music provides an important outlet for stress and contemplation, allowing you to go back into your daily life refreshed. For yet others, you might discover how to meditate, how to connect with the mysterious flow of the Universe when you are immersed in a song. Once you recognize the beauty of that for what it is, you can then learn to connect with the flow in other ways at other times.

We are not suggesting you will find all of your answers in this book. We are, though, inviting you to look at something you love with new eyes, a new perspective, and a new heart. Once you recognize the importance of feeling good in one area of your life, you are open to feeling good in the rest of your life. And that is the cornerstone to mastering your life.

Happy reading!

Meg Bertini

Meg Bertini
Publisher

To John: You are my rock.
Without you I wouldn't be in this happy place in my life.
I used to say "happiness is irrelevant as long as
I'm alive," but this isn't strictly true.

Since I've known you,
I know happiness (and it is good, good).
I also know my truth, the loneliness is gone,
and you have got me singing again
after a long hiatus.

You deserve the Greatest Spouse Award
for putting up with me!

Acknowledgements

I must first thank Meg Bertini and the rest of the DreamTime team for making this book happen. You are such an understanding and creative group of talented people. Thank you for such a wonderful opportunity.

Of course, I give great thanks to John, my spiritual husband and life partner. Without him this book never would have happened. He allows me to see myself with a correct lens. He supports me when I don't support myself. I'm often not kind to myself about myself. I lose direction sometimes and John keeps me on track. Thank you, John-boy. You are my sweet.

I also must give thanks to my mother and father, Lois and Stanley Ennis. Without them I wouldn't have the voice that allows me to sing a hoot or two or I wouldn't have this physical life in which to sing that hoot. My family sadly knows that these are my mother's last years, as she suffers from the debilitating condition of dementia. Without Mom's motherly devotion to me I would have no hope, no sweetness in my heart. She was very good to me and taught me respect and humility. Without my father? Oh my gosh, my life would be so blank. He taught me how to laugh, how to see the world with a fresh eye, and *never* to give up.

I would not be complete without my children, Jacob and Jessyca. I sang to them often as they were growing up. Music was a mainstay in our household during the cold winter months in Minnesota. Jacob, I hope you someday get back to your music. You are a magician with words and also a gifted musician. Don't deny it! I've heard you. And, Jessyca, please pursue your dance again. You are more talented than you know and have a lot to offer others with your style and movement. I love you both, your beautiful spouses Kate and Omar, and my grandbaby, Benicio. He is so very special to me . . . and that salsa dance of his is primo!

Thanks also to my sister, Sarah. You have been a great supporter for my work and an inspiration to me with your vocal gifts. Thank you, Amanda, for being so sweet. May you succeed always in whatever you pursue in your life. To all of their extended family, I wish you happiness and thanks for being there.

Thank you to all of my wonderful friends and clients all over the world. I am so blessed to have met so many people and taken part in all your stories and life experiences. And thank you to Mother Earth for providing such a beautiful land (thank you for raining endlessly for days on end so I'd sit to get this book done!). To all the wonderful animal and plant life that graces my path. And to all the wonderful teachers and mentors I've had throughout time . . . I thank you.

Singing Meditation

Music is a moral law. It gives soul to the universe,
wings to the mind, flight to the imagination,
and charm and gaiety to life and to everything.

—PLATO

Virtually every person has caught himself or herself singing from time to time—at least when no one else is listening! We all have the delightful need to provide harmony to the music around us. Our prose is song. Language should always flow into a melody.

Singing doesn't need to be professional, or even pleasant to the ear, to be beneficial to the well-being of the person performing. The very process of intonating a few phrases of a song can help a person begin to mend the spiritual connection between the physical material world and the invisible heartfelt dimensions of the soul. Whether you sing a song for sixpence, six dollars, or only for your own enjoyment, it makes no difference to the soul.

It's my intention in this book to get everyone, regardless

of ability, to sing from the deepest part of their beings, as a devotional to life. Sing to honor the creative force that provides us life. Perhaps, if we all start singing, we will generate a peace unlike anything this earth has seen since before humanity walked upon it. Mother Nature is a song all on her own. It's time we started to sing along to a song, replacing discord with the unity of a common theme. Instead of just a national anthem, let's sing a world anthem of love!

We could each begin by picking a song that resonates with us personally, and then expand into singing the song chosen by another, and then another . . . and so on. Soon there will be many songs being sung at once. It will begin to sound like a chorus, and then, eventually, become one song sung by many. It will sound like one voice.

The power of music and singing is that it preoccupies everything: mind, body, and soul. It demands attention as it rejuvenates the spirit. When one is singing, singing becomes the focus. If we all focus on singing for positive influence for our souls, then our creation will become a unified effort, which eventually brings goodness to all.

I hope that by telling my personal stories about music and singing I will inspire other individuals to sing their songs as well. I am by no means a professional singer. Yes, I have had some vocal training in the past; I have sung a song or two in front of the public, but only as an amateur. I don't have a perfectly trained voice and am certain that at times when I sing those who hear me would like to tape my mouth shut! I can be off-key and shaky when I sing, especially in front of others, but that's not the point of this book.

If I were teaching professional singing, I'd need many years of training and practice. I don't have the time to go that route, so I just want to share the treasures that singing has brought to my world. I'll do that by way of telling my story about music, singing, and the ways it has embellished my life.

Here's how the book is structured: In most chapters, I'll tell you a story, share a personal experience from my life, say something about music and singing. I will then describe the quality that this experience brought into my life. For instance, when I used to sing in the church choir, I always felt a sense of reverence. It was my weekly devotional time. It was also the time that I could relieve my guilt over the transgressions I had committed in the previous week. So in that case, I'll discuss the quality of reverence within this chapter, and how reverence is necessary to the life of a good soul.

I will also discuss how that particular quality can add a dimension to your life as a body-mind-and-spirit being on this planet, and I'll follow up in some cases with a meditation on the specific quality that I call *The Singing Meditation*.

Most chapters include personal experiences of my own related to singing or listening to the songs; most of them also represent qualities that the experiences gave me, how the reader might find and nourish those qualities within him or her, and visualizations (a meditation exercise) that will help the reader integrate the qualities. Finally, later on in the book, I'll discuss rhythms and techniques to improve vocal quality, confidence, and pitch to ensure that the hobbyist gets the most out of singing!

ABOUT SOUL QUALITIES

Music and rhythm find their way
into the secret places of the soul.

—PLATO

I cannot begin to think of music without thinking about soul attributes. Music brings us to our souls.

My view of "soul" is that it refers to the individual breath of life, the inner psyche expressed through our personalities as people. Each one of us has a unique soul identity or pattern (made up of life experiences, memory, personality traits, preferences and personal connection to a larger force outside of self, possibly the Divine) that inter-prets life on an inner plane of awareness. It is personal to the individual and exhibited to others through self-expres-sion and experience.

If you were to examine music or songs that you like, their content would tell you a lot about who you are as a person. This type of examination might tell you exactly what is inside of you at a soul level, and how to bring out more of those soul qualities in your life. For example, whenever I am feeling somewhat in charge of my world, I listen to Bach. This puts me in touch with the powerful, strong side of myself. It reinforces my confidence.

In the past, when I'd search for the ambitious side of myself, or the motivated part within me, I would listen to the group Heart's 1985 album, *Heart.* I especially used the songs *If Looks Could Kill* and *What About Love* to get my heart pumping. Today, I might listen to a little rap music to get my blood moving. Aerobic exercise is *all* about the music, right? This type of music shows me the ambitious, creative side of my soul personality.

For the softer side, the romantic within me, I might listen to some Nat King Cole . . . or perhaps some older country music, if I wanted to cry a little! If I want to feel my feminine side, I have a whole list of women songwriters/singers I can get into and with whom I can dance. And then, some of today's artists, like Clay Aiken or Jack Johnson, really set the mood for love. In *this* category, the list is endless!

As you can see, each type of music, every song out there, and especially the artists themselves, can bring out different qualities from deep within our soul-hood. We're all together in soul, even if we have various views on how to get there— religions, philosophies, psychologies and, as suggested in this book, our hobbies . . . like singing.

I don't care how awful you might think your voice is; who is it going to hurt if you sing when you're alone? Besides, why should we care what other people think? As long as we are respectful of other people's space, it shouldn't bother anyone if we sing, sing, sing, to our heart's content!

SAMPLE SINGING MEDITATION

Position yourself in a chair or on the floor, sitting as comfortably as you can. Imagination can help you here: it's simply the mind's creative energy, and the more positive you make your thoughts, the better you will feel—and the better results you will have. The imagination can have positive results in terms of singing, too.

So—close your eyes, sit up straight, take a deep breath, and then release it. Now imagine that out in front of you are two notes.

Once you can see these notes clearly in your imagination, begin to hum them. Now try and see another note. Take a deep breath, and begin to sing an *ahhhhh* sound to this note. And now an *ohhhhh* sound to the note . . .

Now begin to visualize several notes in front of you. Begin to sing *la, la, la,* to these notes. As the notes start coming to you in your imagination, continue to sing the *la* sound. *La, la, la* . . . on and on. You're singing from your imagination!

Now begin to sing, *one, two, three,* to the notes appearing in your imagination. Next, imagine that you only see one note, but still sing *one, two, three* or *A, B, C,* to the same note. It will come out as a monotone, like a chant.

Play around with the music as it comes to you. If you don't see or hear any music, that's fine. You may want to eliminate the visualization exercises—or just practice this visualization more often. Eventually something will come to you.

This is how we do the singing meditation. The visualizations will change according to the issue or the quality sought. Now, begin to sing a song that you love to sing. If you don't sing very often, *make up* a song that you love to sing. This will become your own personal song—just for you!

ONE

Singing for Your Soul

We must begin to make what I call "conscious choices,"
and to really recognize that we are the same.
It's from that place in my heart that I write my songs.

—JOHN DENVER (1943–1997)

Here on the ground, our job is not done.

—JAMES BROWN, THE "GODFATHER OF SOUL"
(1933–2006)

I am a professional psychic consultant and trainer. I work with people as a counselor, confidante, and teacher. I use my abilities as a psychic intuitive to help others navigate through their lives by glimpsing what might be coming for them in the future, and by looking into a past that might still be producing discomfort.

What this means is that I have natural abilities to see beyond what is obvious to most of us. We've all experienced intuition of some sort (see Appendix E, Intuitive Hunches and Song)—why do you sometimes choose Street B instead of Street A, or know who is calling you on the phone? Something inside just tells you. That is your *intuition*.

A psychic has very refined intuitive abilities—and more: a sixth sense that can foretell the future and analyze the past. This ability, combined with my counseling skills and relational skills, allows me to help people in ways others cannot by offering insight and techniques to my clients. I often tell them to sing a song, or write a song to sing, as this helps in the healing process and leaves something they can review later.

I've worked with people all over the world in very many different occupations and life situations. My work with clients is confidential, and changes from each session as to what material will be discussed and used. It is a very challenging yet rewarding vocation, and I treat my work and clients with the utmost respect.

I'm going to use my knowledge, gifts and skills as a psychic advisor to explain why it's helpful to bring music and the gift of song into play to make for a better life as soulful beings on this planet. Not only is singing a hobby, it often becomes my refuge when things become stressful or painful in my day-to-day life. Singing helps: it's become a form of meditation. I also use visualization and vocal technique to improve the *quality* of my singing.

HOW VISUALIZATION IS USED IN THIS BOOK: THE SINGING MEDITATION

I am always encouraging people to center themselves, to "get quiet" in their own minds. The best way to do this is to meditate.

Any form of quieting the mind can be a meditation. Sometimes people go to monasteries or on retreats to meditate far away from their normal routines. But in our busy world, most people only have short periods throughout the day— and usually only at home—to spend any time at all quieting the mind.

It's not easy to shut off the thinking process, or to transition from a hectic schedule into a mode of calm. Music can be a great bridge for slowing down the mind and relaxing the body. Singing is a doorway into music; it brings you to that bridge. Pick a song that you like to sing, whether on the radio or a CD; or just sing *a cappella* (without instrumentation, just using your voice), and begin to sing with as much passion as you can!

After you've been singing for a while, think about how it makes you feel. Individual songs create different sensations in the body.

When you've finished the song, and have noticed how it makes you feel, then concentrate on the feeling or the experience the song opened up for you. Perhaps it has memories attached to it from your past. Or maybe the song's lyrics have a powerful message you can meditate upon. Just contemplate whatever the song brings up for you.

What feelings does the song bring out in you? Do you feel peace, prosperity, sadness, truth? Does it generate a sense of sincerity or triumph? Any number of feelings can be found in one song. That's the intention of many songwriters; they want their songs to generate a range of emotions within the listener or singer. Open yourself to these feelings: singing can be your meditation. Sing with passion; discover the feelings elicited by singing certain songs and contemplate the qualities that they create inside you.

If you sing a song every day with this type of focus, it becomes a singing meditation, and can bring deep joy into your life. Vocalizing—as you do when you sing a song—can enliven even the most sedentary soul. Have you ever been in a nursing home when schoolchildren are giving a concert? Most of the residents love the music and truly come to life during these moments. Singing is a universal language.

Research has shown meditation lowers heart rate and blood pressure, and singing can be a form of meditation that is healthy and accessible to many. In my work as a psychic/spiritual counselor, I teach people how to use the power of the mind to create and correct things in their lives. Much of this work is done with *visualization*, the use of imagination to see things in the mind before they happen in reality.

LEARNING TO VISUALIZE

Everyone has an imagination. We all see things in our mind's eye. Yet many of us have been told that what we can imagine is not real, and never will be. Forget all that for these exercises in visualization! Visualization can help a body heal. It helps athletes perform better. It helps people calm down or cheer up.

Structured visualization is simply taking something we are working on in our life and creating an imaginary experience from that. This will lead us to different perceptions about the situation, or give us ideas of ways to change it. It usually has a positive outcome.

I take my clients a bit further than just visualizing situations as they would like them to be; I help them become comfortable with situations as they are in the present, and then add things to the visualization to help the situation change in the future.

One of the ingredients I like to add to these pictures is *light* in different colors, quantities, and textures. Light is all around us. Light defines the shadows. When you're in a dark room, a flashlight or lamp will define what is in the room with you. When you are imagining a situation, light can illuminate reasons, causes for the situation. Light can often alter the outcome of a situation: when you understand the causation of a situation, you can feel differently about it, perceive it in a different light. Blend the light with your favorite song and you have a meditation that will lift your spirits.

In some of the chapters I relay my experiences involving specific types of music and different songs. Each of these musical experiences created a sensation inside me that helped bring my life to a wonderful place. I discuss those sensations and point to how you, too, can attain the same feelings through music and visualization. Use your imagination, close your eyes, and listen to what I am talking about in the meditation exercises.

For instance, if we are talking about love, I might have you imagine a meeting with a wonderful angel or a person you love. You would bring them closer to you in your imagination and begin to feel the quality of love within your being. I might also have you surround yourself and this other person with light in your visualization, just bringing the good sensation of light to the relationship. This is how we will elevate your experience through the use of music and visualization.

You can do the visualization while listening to your favorite meditation music. This could help produce the chapter's target quality and it may alter your life—even to the extent that you will want to do visualization on a regular basis! If it does nothing for you, then disregard the meditations—and sing the music anyway!

AN INTERVIEW WITH SONGWRITER/ SINGER LISA GERMANO

Lisa Germano began her professional singing career as a backup singer and fiddle player for John Mellencamp; she's worked with many other artists and bands over the years. She writes her own music and completed her first opera when she was seven years old. Her piano and vocal ballads are hauntingly real. "I've learned to find beauty in the sad places," Lisa explains. By singing about such things "they're not so devastating."

Lisa says she's not always been comfortable with her own voice. "I *wanted* to like my voice, but I didn't for a long time." She points to how soft it is, but I've heard her in concert, and although her voice *is* soft, it is also very powerful, and it helps her to tell detailed stories in her songs.

I asked Lisa what she would recommend to a novice

singer. "Pick an easy song that you like and sing it, just begin to sing it." If a person wants to learn to sing well, "then practice the easy songs over and over again."

What else? "Pick ten favorite songs and practice. Don't believe any particular rules about singing, and just do what works for you. Get to know your voice first, and then get instruction if you need it."

Lisa tells me that she now finds her own voice very soothing, and when she has the jitters before a performance, her anxiety eases as soon as she begins to sing. Find that softness within your own voice and sing. It might ease the stress in *your* life, as well!

When I asked about songwriting and how Lisa finds the inspiration for particular songs, she responded that "being open for it to come" is the most important. "You have to be self-disciplined and then—" she paused a moment "—honoring it when it comes. It just happens."

I imagined her getting inspiration and allowing it to happen. This inspired me. Lisa's music continues to enchant audiences worldwide, and she accomplishes her stated goal of connecting with her listeners—she certainly did with me when I was a member of her audience. Lisa gives us a lot to think about and feel. Her songs are very moving and motivational.

Lisa's most recent album, *In The Maybe World*, is a compilation of her past compositions (lisagermano.com). For me, her music is sweet and sour, beautiful . . . and sometimes dark. It leads you into the examination of the soul, as it did for her when she wrote the songs, as good music always does.

TWO

Music as My Muse

I don't know anything about music.
In my line you don't have to.
ELVIS PRESLEY (1935–1977)

Music is a grand experience in and of itself. Harmonics and vibration can create all kinds of wonderful sensations. I've loved music since I was very young, back when I sat in front of the television singing along to the bouncing ball of Mitch Miller.

It wasn't until I began to study the mind, metaphysics, and healing, that I began to notice how beneficial (or even how harmful) music can be to a person's well-being. We forget to play music when we need a boost, and—even worse— we forget to turn it off when it's interfering with our happiness.

I've also found that singing or chanting can bring about a positive shift in my health, mood, and attitude. This is where I reflect on my life, looking at the periods when singing became very important to me as a hobby and (as a child) a fantasy dream career. I remember parts of my life related to music and its encouraging effects, and how "letting it all out" through singing has boosted my consciousness. I'm always advising people to find their favorite song on the radio and sing along. It lifts the spirit and rejuvenates the soul.

As I mentioned before, I began to "sing along with Mitch" as a child. For those of you too young to remember, Mitch Miller was a well-known recording artist and producer. He directed a male chorus that sang on his television show, *Sing Along with Mitch,* once a week back in the early 1960s.

I sat very close to the TV and sang the words along with the ball that bounced on the words on the screen as they were to be sung. It delighted me to hear the songs coming to life from my own throat, sung by my own voice. I also sang a lot to my imaginary friends and invisible crowds while I was tucked away alone in my bedroom. What child hasn't dreamed of performing on stage just like her favorite singer?

As I got a little older, I became shy about singing where anyone could hear me. My mother was tone-deaf, but she loved music. She would encourage me to sing often, but I wasn't comfortable being the center of attention.

When I was in fifth grade, however, all of that changed. I was accepted into the elementary school choir. *Wow! What an impossible feat,* I remember thinking. I was very pleased with myself, and my parents were quite proud of me.

Something very strange occurred, however, at our first public performance. My body rocked so hard to the music that the director asked my parents where I'd learned to move like that while singing! They had no idea, and they later mentioned to me that I might like to "tone it down a bit" when performing. But when I was singing a song, my entire being was involved. I just couldn't be that disciplined, at least not until I was a little older.

I should explain my high school concert choir. I grew up in a small, rural Midwestern town, and the high school was significant in size. It was the only one for miles around, so class sizes were bigger than those in most city schools: our class had close to four hundred students! So to get into the concert choir was quite an achievement. The choir was made up of around ninety students from grades eleven and twelve; a little over ten percent of those who wanted to be in the choir were selected to participate. To me this was an absolute dream come true.

Being accepted into the concert choir was one of the highest honors I ever received. It meant day after day of practicing and learning how to make my voice do what it must to perform in public venues. My timidity was hidden by the fact that there were other students on stage with me, and I was in the third row from the back. I was never asked to sing a solo because I could never get up the courage. I just didn't have it in me then, but I did love the stage, and I have always loved to sing.

When I was raising my own children I always had music playing in our home. Television was not a regular mode of entertainment; records were. And I'd built up quite a collection! As a teenager I became obsessed with buying any new song on the market on 45s—or "vinyl," as they call it today. I had boxes and boxes of records.

I would save my allowance and any earned cash until I had enough to get the weekly top-ten single or a longer album. I would sit in my room playing the songs over and over again until I had every word of the lyrics memorized. Often I would play one line, write down the words, and then put the needle back onto the record for the next line. Once I had all the words written down, I'd begin to sing the song over and over until I had it firmly lodged in my memory bank.

The next step was to match my voice perfectly to the artist performing the song. I was a copy-cat junkie! It was very important to me to recognize inflections in the voice and qualities in the music that created a sensation in my body.

And I still do that today. A crooner's vocals might create a sense of passion or romance in my body, while a rapper might unleash a wilder side of the emotion, a sense of urgency or power. I pay attention to my body and the way it feels while a song is playing.

Music has become my muse: it inspires me while it helps me externalize my feelings. A good ol' country love ballad may have me crying in my shoes, whereas a lively bit of baroque music may have my head in the clouds. I pay attention to my mood and play the appropriate music, or I play the appropriate music to help generate a mood I'd like to be in.

When my children were small and prone to being grumpy, I would throw on an Oak Ridge Boys tune to get them a-singin' and a-dancin'. What fun! *Bobbie Sue* became the run-around-and-jump-off-the-couch song and *Elvira* got the fannies moving. Such delightful memories!

Today, as grown-ups, my children harbor doubts as to whether they were ever so carefree as to move to such silly music, but I remember it well.

So what I'm attempting to show here is that singing can be very positive for your well-being. Music is magic. Music is the muse.

In most chapters where I describe a quality that a song produced within my experience, we will move more fully into the quality via the use of visualization in a meditative state. Don't worry if you have difficulty meditating, for visualizing is a fun way to relax the body and mind. Whatever you get, you get. It is your reality, and no one else's, in these moments. If nothing else, turn on the radio and visualize. Enjoy the music. Enjoy singing until your heart is content. It is my hope that by the end of this book you will feel wonderful and take that joy out into the world with you to share with others. Joy is contagious, and in this case music is the catalyst.

I hope to inspire you to sing, regardless of what your voice sounds like. In the next chapter we'll work on perfection. Almost everyone can improve their voice with concentration and listening. In later chapters, we'll work on vibration and harmony. This is where you might begin to feel how the voice can flux and change the music. Blending with others or with a song on the radio can be done by hitting the same note, or by chording (hitting a note that is in the same chord as the front vocal; it's the same thing as harmonizing.)

Remember, I am not a professional. I just feel the music and love to sing. It is my hobby, but sometimes I get lucky and get to sing with the pros. I've learned a lot by listening and by "letting it out" through song. You can, too! Let's begin our journey of singing: your soul is waiting.

A STORY OF THE SIRENS AND PANDORA

I've long been fascinated by two myths: the sirens of the sea, and Pandora's box. The sirens were nymph-like creatures (half-woman, half-bird; in modern versions, the sirens are likened to mermaids), muses of the sea that lived on the cliffs and rocks of an island. As sailors approached, the sirens sang and played enchanting music, mesmerizing the

sailors so that their boats crashed into the rocks and they drowned.

Pandora was the first woman, created by Zeus as Prometheus's punishment for stealing fire from the gods and giving it to humanity. All the deities gave Pandora (the meaning of her name is "all gifts")—well, *gifts*. She had the same power, strength and beauty as the gods.

In addition, Zeus himself gave her a storage jar filled with a mysterious gift. She was told to never open the jar, but curiosity overcame her. When she opened it, all kinds of evils were released into the world. She closed the jar before she released *hope*. And for a time, the world was a very bleak place, with ill fortune everywhere, but finally Pandora opened the jar again and hope was released. Now humanity always has hope in the midst of hard times.

If the siren song is resisted or just listened to in passing and Pandora's box is left alone, we can enjoy their music and the mystery all the same. These stories intrigue me because I am always seeking the alluring things in life.

Music can have a hypnotic effect, and often I've had to discipline myself to leave the radio or stereo to get other things accomplished. I am a fan of improvisational music, jazz, blues, classical, rock, country, and to some degree now hip-hop. I find the sounds, the rhythms, the harmonies compelling and want to sing my way into heaven. I imagine the siren song to be very melodic and filled with passion. I want to open Pandora's box just to make sure there is nothing more in there. Balancing hope and self-control is the way to avoid being seduced by curiosity and deceit!

The Siren's Muse and Pandora's Secret

A poem by Jules

T'was on the sea they set to sail, the siren's voice they heard.

A moan, a groan a pleasant wail, innocence now being lured.

Pandora's box intrigues them so, but nothing do they find.

A gentleman's search both high and low, mysteries misplace
the mind.

Within the box a secret kept, the yowling tempt as well.

Regret with these of course they wept, embarrassed they
shall not tell.

Is it true, o' grand one, virginity fair; Pandora of beauty,
sirens of call.

They place their faith in someone there, when heed they
should not trust at all.

Find the mysteries so deep and dark, Pandora's box or
siren's muse.

In seductive decoy is found the lark, how many more will
succumb to ruse?

Reprieve this moment the maidens dear, to reveal a
temptress in waiting.

Singing to the water so bright and clear, to kill with such
vicious placating.

Pandora's silence is the siren's call, but neither must we fear.

Need we listen to hope after all, and pass on by, with cheer.

The story is written, the song has been sung; to repeat the fate
would be at death's toll. The meaning is left for the human
tongue; the lesson learned must come from the soul.

THREE

Choir, Chorus, and Church Lofts

To sing like this, in the company of other souls, and to make those consonants slip out so easily and in unison, and to make those chords so rich that they bring tears to your eyes. This is transcendence. This is the power that choral singing has that other music can only dream of.

—Garrison Keillor

I've always been somewhat of a lonely soul. When I was young I didn't play much with the other children. I was raised a Catholic, and that, along with the fact that I wasn't the type to truly "act out" (just wasn't in my nature), meant that I followed the rules pretty closely. But there was always something missing in my life.

In junior high school I began to sing behind closed doors. I would buy records, copy the lyrics, and sing along with the music. Some of the music I liked didn't seem to fit the religious theme of my household's faith, so I began to deviate and explore. By the time I had hit tenth grade, I had developed a growing fascination with singing: anything, anywhere, anytime . . . except alone in public. I had limited self-confidence in my singing abilities in front of people, but I absolutely loved being in vocal groups. So I took part in three during my high school years: a full eighty-person concert choir at the high school; an all-girls chorus, also at the high school; and my favorite (because of the loft, the organ, and the Wednesday-night practices), the church choir.

The full choir was the large eighty-member concert choir in my high school. Everyone who had any interest in singing tried out for this choir. Roger Tenney, the director, was well known in my small town. He had taken his choir to Washington, DC, several years before, to sing in front of the president of the United States, because he'd been named National Teacher of the Year in 1967. After that, *everyone* in the school wanted to participate in his choir!

I was fortunate to be chosen to sing in two of his choirs in the years between 1972 and 1975, an all-girl chorus and the full choir. Roger Tenney was a perfectionist; there was absolutely no time for dilly-dallying in his choir. Chewing gum was definitely a no-no: choristers who didn't deposit their gum in the trash basket immediately upon entering were reprimanded. Roger had an incredible ear for harmonics; his blending of voices was impeccable.

First came the solo audition. When I first auditioned for the concert choir, he advised me that I had a good voice. I had the ability to belt out a song, but my confidence was hampered by fear. I was then placed in the girl's chorus. I needed practice until I could sing solo in front of a group without my voice wavering.

In my final year of high school, I became a member of the

concert choir. Even though this was a great honor, I also had a lot of fun and learned a lot about harmony, teamwork, and vocalizing.

Roger Tenney's passion for excellence, coupled with my own drive and desire to be a part of this collaboration, were daunting. To make my task even more difficult, after the audition process—and once the choir was chosen—it was still not a sure thing that everyone would remain a permanent member.

The first few weeks of putting this new group together were very detailed and required the utmost of patience from the members and the director. Roger would take a voice and begin matching it with others. There were two rows of altos, tenors, sopranos and basses.

Much of the work for the existing concert choir members was robotic, as they'd been in the choir for a year by the time I joined. They knew the material and could sing much of the music without any difficulty. Coming on board as a senior was very demanding and often frightening for me, but it was also a driving challenge. I struggled to read music, but found that my colleagues were more than willing to help me. I also struggled with the ability to hear myself when standing between others singing different notes. Often I would cover one ear in an effort to hear whether I was on key or not.

My part was determined to be alto: I sing comfortably from my throat at a deeper tone, which is alto. I can also use my falsetto voice at higher range. A falsetto voice is an unnatural or artificially high-pitched voice that comes from the head. It's still my voice, but there's a different resonance when I sing very high notes as opposed to lower notes. Plus

I have a range of notes in between that are difficult to sing.

In the choir, I was placed in the back row of the two rows of alto singers. Behind me were two rows of tenors (high male voices). The front row of the tenors sat behind me. My voice was perfectly matched by Director Tenney to the alto on my left, the alto on my right, the tenor behind me and the alto in front of me.

Not only did he blend the choir that way, but at times he mixed us up so that we would have soprano (highest female voice), alto, bass (lowest male voice) and tenor combinations all throughout the choir. It was a very involved process, but one that I relished; I was so proud to be a part of something so complex. There was great perfection in this methodology of choir development: I was a part of something much bigger than myself. This was a team effort and a great example of excellence in action.

GIRLS CHORUS

Let me tell you now about my experience of being a part of the girls chorus. Although we were still under the direction of Roger Tenney, he did have a student assistant director. This choir could not take precedence for Roger, as the senior choir came first. Yet it was his creation, and I sensed it was a place where he could let go and enjoy himself. And he did smile and have fun. He allowed us to do things in the girls chorus that the concert choir, because of its necessary perfection, could not experience.

I also made some truly incredible friendships in that group. We had a lot of fun. We worked hard. We blended our voices by ourselves. We loved the music we sang. It was excellent practice for the full choir later on.

The girls chorus was allowed to be funky, foolish, and free with the music. In that there was another kind of perfection, the sort that comes from camaraderie and true human unity. We made the audience laugh. We enjoyed the music and yet we were very serious about performing it well. Being a part of a group of females this large, blending voices to make one, is an archetypal experience for sure. Girls chorus was a beautiful way to make music!

CHURCH CHOIR

During these same years, I was asked by my piano instructor to join the church choir. Jean Leonard was the director of and organist for the choir. The organ was magnificent and the choir loft overlooked the congregation seated below. At age fifteen, I was the youngest member of the choir, and stayed until I turned twenty-one. The oldest member of the choir was in her eighties and had sung in choirs since her youth. Her vocal cords had changed as she aged, though I could tell that once upon a time, she had possessed a most splendid voice.

There was no perfection of matching voices in *this* choir! Out of the twenty or so members, we had only two male members. Many of the voices were a bit off-key, but everyone shared in their spirit and service to congregation in those hours of practice and performance. In that way, the disarray of vocal blending was another kind of perfection.

The church choir allowed anyone with the willingness

and passion to join. What touched me most was the beauty of the architecture that surrounded us on our Wednesday night practices. I sometimes arrived an hour early, climbed the creaking wooden staircase, and knelt at the edge of the loft, looking down over the entire church. It was dark in the loft, save for a small light above the organ. I felt so reverent in those moments. I sang my praises in silence as I leaned over that balcony rail. It was my time to contemplate and feel safe.

Singing in the church choir in the loft was a very reverent, perfect time in my life. The quality in all three of these group activities that I felt within myself, in very different ways, was perfection.

> Musical training is a more potent instrument than any other, because rhythm and harmony find their way into the inward places of the soul, on which they mightily fasten.
>
> —PLATO

THE QUALITY OF PERFECTION

Having said that, however, I have to state my belief that nothing is perfect. I always say that perfection comes through accepting our flaws, but that we all have an idea of what perfection could be. For me, being in the three types of vocal singing groups, all at the same time in my life, brought about a sense of perfection. Everything in those moments of performance was precisely sequential. That's what perfection is to me.

Think about what perfection is to *you*.

Visualize: Close your eyes. Take a deep breath in, and

release it. You may play music in the background if you like. Begin to feel what perfection could feel like in your body. Do not try to arrange the ideas of your experience or situations in your life at this moment into perfection. Just imagine what perfection must feel like.

Imagine that you see dots of light in front of you. Observe closely what these dots look like. Are they dark, are they multi-colored? Are there many dots? Perhaps you only have a single dot or several dots in front of you? Take the dots and arrange them so that they are perfect in your estimation. Bring the dots into perfect alignment.

You have the dots in front of you now, in perfect alignment. Now imagine that these dots represent parts of your life. Can you tell which dot represents another person? Which one is a situation? See if these dots have more infor-

mation for you. If they do, you might write down what you perceive from this exercise.

When you finish the exercise, you may open your eyes and sing a song or play some music. Then close your eyes again and see what the dots do and where they go with music. There is perfection. Let's all sing in perfect harmony!

AN INTERVIEW WITH ROGER TENNEY

Roger Tenney began his career in 1942 directing choirs in the army as a minister of music. He spent two years in the military directing vocal groups for all faiths during religious services. He then went on to direct school choirs, including the choirs in which I sang, and was music teacher and director of choirs at the high school in Owatonna, Minnesota, for thirty-two years.

In 1967 he was named National Teacher of the Year the first-ever music teacher to be nominated and given this award. He took his concert choir to Washington, DC, where they sang for President Lyndon Johnson at the White House. Roger gave lectures in forty-six states after he won this award. His teaching methods were an inspiration to high school music programs everywhere.

He claims that when he began his teaching career at the Owatonna High School in 1960 there were thirty-eight women and only twelve men who signed up for the choir. He told the ladies that if they didn't bring seventeen more men in, he'd drop one half of the women. They frantically went up and down the halls of the high school and dragged males into the choir, and Roger Tenney's concert choir began its first year with success.

In 1961 he took the choir to a competition at the Minnesota State Fair and won first place. In 1962, the choir represented Minnesota in Seattle at a national competition. Roger began recruiting choir students early on by taking the existing high school choir into the elementary schools, allowing the big kids, the "important" kids (like captains of football teams, etc.) to show the younger students that music (and choir in particular) was a great activity in which to be involved. It was a winning campaign.

I've always liked harmony, where each voice blends with the next. When I asked Roger how he blended or matched the voices of his choirs, he said, "You just listen. You take sections of the choir, find the tone that you want and begin to match it." He remarked that the students then begin to "imitate one another" and it becomes virtually "mechanical," where all four or eight parts are working in sync with each other. His favorite part of directing is "interpreting a phrase line that is musical."

Every year Roger listened to the voices of each eighth grade student in the city to begin recruiting students for high school choral groups. He found that many students didn't think they could sing because someone in their lives had told them they couldn't. "Everyone can sing," he suggests, "all you need to do is *believe* you can sing."

Even though long-retired from high school choir directing, Roger Tenney still directs choirs today for various performances and is always active in music. Thank you, Roger, for inspiring so many young people to sing!

FOUR

Hope, Trust, and Honor

Hope is the thing with feathers that perches in the soul,
and sings the tune without words, and never stops at all.

—EMILY DICKINSON

I BELIEVE—HOPE

Over the years as a devoted daughter, wife, mother, counselor, and now a grandmother, I have known that before
anything else, there must be hope. In order to pull oneself
out of a state of depression and hopelessness, there must be
hope.

From hope we go to belief. First we hope that what we
long for is out there. Then, as we move into hope, we start to
believe that what we need and want is, in fact, out there.
Once we believe, we must have faith that *what* we believe
and hope for will come.

Spirituality gives us belief in powers beyond what we can
see, touch, feel and hear. It gives us belief that something
larger exists. I was eleven years old when I first heard the

song *I Believe* performed by Sandler and Young. Young sang *I Believe,* and Sandler sang the *Ave Maria* as part of a synchronized duet in a very beautiful rendition of the song. (*I Believe* was written in 1952 by Ervin Drake, Irvin Graham, Jimmy Shirl, and Al Stillman.)

The lyrics suggest that whenever we are led astray, there will always be someone that comes along to show us the right way. How many times in my life have I gone astray? Way too many to count. Even though as a child I did my very best *not* to break any of the rules that I'd been taught, I was still a child. As a teenager I was gone on the *stray* a lot, and as an adult somewhat more so.

When we're young, we forget that there are powers beyond our small existence. But every single time I was led astray, there was someone, somehow, who came to me and pulled me back onto the right path. It may have been a television program; sometimes it was a good friend or even a stranger. Sometimes I go in search of these people, and sometimes I let them find me.

I went through a desolate time when I was in my early thirties. I know that for many this incident will seem petty, but for me it was a life-or-death situation. I was emotionally distraught, searching for something. I had lost my job and felt I had no power or control because of my limited finances. Other things contributed to my depression, and I was feeling very much alone. I had two small children who depended on me for their spiritual growth and physical needs, so I was unlikely to harm myself; yet I was in crisis.

One day I received a phone call from a woman I didn't know—a stranger. She told me that her name was Susan and explained that someone had told her I was looking for a way to improve my life, a way to enlighten myself. As distressed as I was, I heard something in her voice, and a seed of compassion entered me when I needed it most.

Susan was offering a class—for twenty dollars, within my price range—that might help me add the things that I wanted and needed to have happen.

It was a beam of light in my dark and dreary world. I said, "Yes, I'll attend the class." The next day I received a job offer, one that would allow me to take my children to work with me if they were sick or had days off from school, an important factor at that time. Susan's class turned out to be a life-changing event for me.

This is an instance where someone came along to show me the way. It also reinforced my belief in something much more powerful than me was at work through the synchronicity of another person's life and teaching. The song I Believe also expresses that a baby's cry can bring us, as adults, to the appreciation for our own existence.

There is nothing more incredible in life than birth, except perhaps death. I believe that because I know the special gift of new life. Holding a baby is an incredible experience. When my son was born, I cried all night in praise of the gift I'd been given. When my daughter was born it was again a sleepless, teary night. I was so elated at having such blessings. When my niece was born, I was on the other side of childbirth, happy to help my sister and be present for another sweet young thing's beginning. When my grandson was born . . . oh, my! I was first grateful that my daughter made it through the labor and delivery, and at the same time that I was allowed to be present. This, if nothing else, convinces me to believe.

We exist in the world to help carry it forward. We are the compost that will once again dissolve back into planet Earth. Our spirits live on. As individuals, we go from hope, belief, and faith, to knowing that we are part of a larger Universe. All one has to do is step out into nature and spend some time with a tree or listen to the ocean's roar or breathe in the almost oxygen-less air at the top of a mountain to believe that there is power beyond what we can fathom. Of course I believe, and through life's struggle and beauty I also know *why* I believe.

Quality of Hope

In order to believe in something, you first hope that it exists, or will exist. The quality of hope—or, rather, belief— can create a lot of changes. There are certain songs, certain types of music that can start the quality of hope within you.

Close your eyes. Take a deep breath, and then release it. Begin to see a small child, an infant, in front of you. The baby is crying. It may irritate you that the baby is crying and no one is holding it. Find a blanket, and wrap the child in it. Bring the child into your arms and begin to rock back and forth. You may experience your physical body actually rocking back and forth. When you do this, do you feel contented? Hope is contentment. When you have hope for something, you are content that it is most likely coming to you. When you rock the baby, it feels safe; the baby has hope. When you stop rocking, the baby may once again cry, as then the child's hope is gone.

Begin to see music as something that can rock you and give you hope and contentment. Think of your favorite song and sway a little to that music. It gives you a sense of contentment. When you're dancing to the music, there's not a lot of room for fear or anger; there's only room for life.

You may need to turn on the radio or play your CDs more often. You may need to sing along more frequently than you used to, as singing is the way to create a sensation of hope in your body through your voice. There is joy when you sing. Rock the baby in your imagination until the baby is so contented that it falls asleep. Rock your inner child when you are upset. Sing and rock the body to contentment.

> What a mother sings to the cradle goes
> all the way down to the coffin.
> —HENRY WARD BEECHER

SILENT NIGHT—TRUST

Almost everyone has held a baby. Much of the time, we hold crying babies. I've been blessed with two beautiful children.

My son was a sleepy baby; he slept most of the time. We even had to wake him up for feedings for the first few weeks of his life. It was never any problem getting him to go to sleep at night, or down for naps; he was our sleepy baby.

My daughter, on the other hand, was no sleepy baby. She didn't like to sleep and was often fussy. At the time I didn't know that she had allergies to many things, including formula. The doctors claimed it was restlessness and fussiness, so we dealt with it. There were many sleepless nights.

I remember one particular Saturday morning my daughter became fussy and I began to rock her in the rocking chair. Even the rocking movement would not satisfy her. I sang lullabies, one after the other, and nothing calmed her. Because I didn't know the words to any other songs, I started singing a Christmas carol. I sang, "silent night . . . all is calm . . ." and she began to quiet. I sang the song over and over, for hours; it was the only thing that was calming her.

With her little head on my shoulder and patting her little back, I sang each verse many times over. Every time I stopped singing, she began fussing. I sang until four o'clock the next morning, when she was finally asleep and I could go off to bed myself.

To this day, when I hear the song *Silent Night,* tears well up in my eyes. Even though that day was very confusing and frustrating for me as a new parent, it was also very rewarding: it helped me to truly bond with my daughter.

When I was a child, my father sang *You are My Sunshine* to me every night just before bedtime. Dad had a decent voice, but he always sang that song with humor. He sang the first verse seriously, but I always knew something silly was about to come. The second verse got slightly silly as he sang about holding his head and crying because his sunshine had disappeared. Verse three was definitely an improvisation. *Boo, hoo, hoo, hoo, hoo, hoo, hoo, hoo, hoo, hoo, hoo* . . . and so on. It always made me laugh. And it always made my friends laugh.

Another of his favorite songs was *Mrs. Murphy's Chowder.* I remember the song starting with a pair of overalls hanging on the line, but in the only recordings I've found, the pants are already in the chowder. Maybe my imagination had them coming off the line, eaten already by a goat and somehow getting into the chowder . . . or perhaps that was Dad's addition to the song.

There was something very soothing about having my father sing silly songs before bedtime, and about having my mother humming big-band music throughout the house all day long, that really built a sense of trust within me. And I'm sure my daughter felt a sense of trust and comfort with my voice singing *Silent Night.* I recently sang this to my one-year-old grandson, and it calmed him too. Trust is an amazing quality to feel.

Quality of Trust

It's very difficult to trust other people if you've been hurt often.

When I engage in counseling sessions with people, I find that trust is one of the most difficult qualities for many people to develop, because we have prime examples of many others out there who should not be trusted, who do deceptive things.

Trust begins at home, in your heart and with yourself. If you can trust yourself, then chances are you will trust others. Remember, though, that many people are not fully developed on an inner plane and so do not trust themselves. When people do not trust themselves, chances are they do things that aren't trustworthy. Take a look at the people in your life and see how self-developed they are. If they are not very much aware of themselves, chances are they will not be as trustworthy as you are—and as you expect of them. But if a person is aware and operating consciously, then chances are you might be able to trust them with more.

You should trust yourself and trust others only as far as they are developed—or trust them in the way that their lives and personalities are geared. We do not all see the same internal picture, and therefore we act/react from the inner pictures that we see.

This brings us to the subject of love. First you must love yourself, then you can begin to trust yourself. Finally you'll be able to know when you cannot trust yourself, giving yourself space for being human (we all have flaws). And the more you love and trust yourself, the less necessary it will be for you to trust others. And yet, ironically, the more you begin to trust others, the more you will understand others and trust them. And the more you love yourself, the more you will love others. That is a given. The more you love yourself and others, the stronger you will become.

THE OLD RUGGED CROSS—HONOR

I feel close to many religions. I was raised Catholic and

have studied many other different philosophies, beliefs, and religions over the years. I never felt close to the Protestant faith until recently, however.

I'd heard the song *The Old Rugged Cross,* written by Reverend George Bennard in 1913. I'd felt its flavor, but it had no real meaning for me until several years ago when my mother became ill. It was necessary for our family to put her into a nursing care facility for a short while after her surgery. She was just down the hall from the room of a family friend, Joyce.

Joyce was in her nineties at that time. She was very spry, very together, and quite a witty woman, but her body was failing. She was on oxygen and could no longer get around on her own. I spent several visits with Joyce while my mother was in this facility, and she told me stories about myself when I was growing up. She remembered these things, even though we hadn't seen each other for over twenty-five years.

Joyce seemed to be a very spiritual woman with a very keen sense of what was going on. She knew people's intentions, even when they seemed to be doing something different. She was somewhat of a black sheep: independent, strong-willed, knew what she wanted . . . and I felt very much connected with her soul and her life. My mother came home from her stay in the nursing care home, but Joyce didn't go back to her home. She passed one winter day a couple of years ago.

It was on a very cold, bleak winter day when I happened to be visiting that the phone rang in my parents' home. It was Joyce's daughter; she asked to speak with me. She told me that her mother had passed and she would like me to sing *The Old Rugged Cross* at her funeral. I felt honored to have been asked, but was definitely scared about singing a song that was so unfamiliar and at such an unfamiliar service.

But because I knew Joyce had such a spirit for life, I accepted. I had two days to practice the song. I downloaded the lyrics from the Internet and went to work. I practiced with the organist at his home. I found that my vocal range was not appropriate for this song, but it certainly struck a chord in my heart. I felt honored to be singing this at Joyce's farewell celebration.

The lyrics of the old cross standing on a "hill faraway" representing all of our human suffering was a bit much for me to accept. I don't necessarily believe in the concepts of sin and shame—or at least not as the old-world Christian view has it. Yet the stories within the faith have a lot of honor, and this song symbolizes that honor.

I took the song to mean that I will exchange my suffering for the glory of spirit and life. The spirit of life is what I felt on that day I sang in tribute to Joyce. She taught me something in those last days of her life. She taught me that we are all connected. She taught me that no matter how much pain she might have been in, she was still willing to laugh and joke about the ways of this world. She had been trapped *in* that nursing home for years, yet she was not trapped *by* it. She shared many quips with me and showed me that no matter how hard things might seem, if you push through it, you will get to the other side. Love life, honor it, respect it. I was taught by this singing-for-Joyce experience to rise above the hatred, the violence, the ugliness of human behavior, and instead see the glory in all of the gifts given to us in this life.

We live in a wondrous place with amazing opportunities. We can choose to see the darkness or the light. Singing this song in tribute forced me to see the sadness in the fact that many people cannot see beyond the dark, but it also allowed me to see the light more clearly and to examine my own heart. To begin living my life as if every day were a rebirth, another opportunity to grow.

I consider myself a believer in many religious/spiritual teachings, for they all resonate the truth. In the Christian tradition it's Jesus who exemplifies the honor of God by taking on the burdens of humanity and showing us another way. In this he chose to be open to a very violent attack against his human life, but his spirit lived on in spite of the abuses against him.

There are many stories of this type of survival across the religions. Buddhists believe that suffering must be transcended. *The Old Rugged Cross* is a grand example of that transcendence. The cross is the emblem, a symbol that suffering can be handed over to a power greater than self. Now, thanks to Joyce's family's request, when I sing that song, it has that effect.

> Buddhism is about changing the mind.
> —DALAI LAMA

We can use all symbolism to rise above our own personal pains and begin to have reverence for life. As a counselor and student of metaphysics, I have come to know that there is no definite boundary between what I'll call the *form* world and the *non-form* world, the world of spirit. We are basically one and the same.

I have received messages from many people who have crossed to the other side, for clients, friends and myself. I have visions of these people in my dreams and in my clair-voyant state, so I know the veils between the worlds are very thin. In order to have the life, the glory that is meant for us, we must open up to all of life—whether we exist in this life in human form, or in another type of dimension. Song can bridge those dimensions.

The harmonies live on forever.

Quality of Honor

When I think of honor, I visualize myself saluting another person with great respect. I see myself nodding my head in honor, kneeling in honor, and singing tribute in honor.

Visualize: Sit quietly, close your eyes, take a deep breath, and release it. To create a sensation of honor in your body, imagine that in front of you and all the way around you are sheets of solid light. You can think of them like bed sheets that are stretched, but make these sheets out of light. Imagine that you are holding two corners, and that someone else is holding the other two corners of the sheet of light. Ask the other person to let go of the corners and whisk the sheet in front of you. Slap it into the wind. You will see in your imagination that your sheet, shaken in the wind, sends out ripples of light as far as your imagination can see.

If you can, imagine many of these sheets, one on top of the other, with a small space in between so that these sheets of light spread out from beneath you all the way above you and on all sides of you. Imagine these sheets of light rippling in the wind and sending off waves of light as far as you can see. Now open your eyes.

You may not know how these imagination techniques work, especially in this case—where sheets of light can make you feel a sense of honor. Certain songs create a sensation of honor. For each person the songs are different, but the feeling of honor is the same. The sheets of light are the same. If you cannot visualize this or connect the reasoning, it's not that important. Just enjoy the music.

FIVE

Amazing Grace

I think music in itself is healing. It's an explosive expression
of humanity. It's something we are all touched by.
No matter what culture we're from, everyone loves music.

—BILLY JOEL

One of my favorite songs is *Amazing Grace*, probably because it's an easy song to sing! It's very well known, and it seems appropriate at many times throughout life.

Grace is such an amazing feeling. We all know when we feel that we are sitting in grace, or when we've been graced with certain qualities . . . a time when everything seems to be going right, moving along just perfectly. Those are moments of grace, times when you may be sitting in solitude and feeling very good about your life, at peace, serene. No need to take any action in that moment, because all is well. Those are moments of humility and grace.

Amazing grace, how sweet the sound. Life can be a difficult journey. Often we're bogged down in emotions and obsessions and cannot see the right path, the necessary action or thought. A simple prayer or a simple song can set things right again.

Many years ago at a time when I had a great ache in my heart, on a whim, I sang the first verse of *Amazing Grace* on my answering machine. I sang the verse and said behind it, "this is Jules, leave a message." I went out for a few hours.

I came home to ten hang-up calls on my answering machine.

The next morning the phone rang and I answered it. A man's voice asked, "Is this the woman who sang *Amazing Grace* on her answering machine?"

"Yes," I said, cringing.

"Well, I sell furnaces. I was randomly making phone calls last night and got your answering machine. I thought that was the most amazing thing I'd ever heard, so I had nine of my coworkers call and listen to your message. That is incredible!"

I thanked him. By the end of the call, my heart had lifted. What a wonderful compliment! Still, I couldn't keep that on my answering machine any longer. The message may have been helpful for ten people, but I felt that it represented too much ego to leave the message that way. So I removed it, opting for the traditional, "leave a message at the tone!"

Amazing Grace tells us that with the power of grace we can believe. Believing within the heart in something beyond ourselves is a grand experience. Singing this song can bring us to that place of reverence and good feeling. Grace *is* amazing. She teaches us humility and sweetness for life.

Amazing Grace is not the only song that exudes grace to

me. *A Broken Wing,* as performed by Martina McBride, helped me through a rough time in my life. It refers to still flying even with a broken wing. It became a motto song for me because I was hurting, but I was still flying. I had my hopes and dreams, and without any earthy attachments I could then pursue those dreams. What a flight this could be! But my wing was still broken. Only with grace could I move forward.

Our dreams may be heavy, especially with a broken wing. And yes, it hurts a lot to fly at times like these, but we can do it. I found a Power bigger than myself and began to sing again. I went for many, many years without singing aloud, except to my babies. When the babies grew up, I stopped singing, and that was my mistake. But now I say, "sing to your heart's content." Crank up the radio and sing along. I no longer have a broken wing. I can fly, fly, fly . . . all because I started singing again. All because I found grace again and have learned to celebrate my life in humility.

We mustn't take life for granted. Stop and smell the roses, and appreciate the fact that we get this opportunity to live in such a beautiful world. Block out the violence and destruction that might be happening outside your front door; overlook it for a short time, look up at the sky. See the sun and the stars as a sign that life goes on everywhere beyond our miniscule planet. We only have now, in this moment, to appreciate what we've been given, what we've been allowed. Regardless of the pain and wretchedness we might feel at times, in this moment we can have peace, and we can sing a song. *Amazing Grace, how sweet the sound.*

Grace is an invisible quality, something like luck. It

appears in a very subtle fashion and it seems somewhat like luck. When you have it, others may say you appear lucky to them. But grace is not a quality that is warranted or deserved. It is not a quality that we come by naturally. As infants we have grace, but as we grow older, we forget that grace is out there for our benefit. We do things to disregard or dishonor it. Grace is a quality that comes when you feel good about yourself and your life, your actions and your thoughts. It comes when everything you do has a quotient of responsibility to the higher good, a sense of ethics or being moral. This is what grace is like. This is when grace will be bestowed on you.

People who walk in grace know that they have the potential for wrongdoing in their hearts. All humans have that side of themselves. We all do wrong at one time or another, but it is the intention to do what is most right for yourself and others that allows grace to enter your life. For the most part, people are good at heart. We only do each other wrong when we are angry or frustrated, when life's circumstances don't go our way. Grace happens when you walk an honorable path, when you feel good about what you've done and are about to do.

Grace can come at any time in a person's life. Some people are able to keep grace alive and well in their lives all the time. And some tend to appear very graceless. Just keep in mind that we were once blind, but now we can see. Once you are aware that grace exists and you deserve to have grace in your life, then you can live your life fully aware and move in graceful motion.

What is humility? An action that is taken after grace enters a person's life. In order to maintain a state of grace, one must be humble in order to keep it. Certainly we have every right to complain when things are not going well in our lives, but to keep the state of grace in place, we walk with humility and give that grace to others by serving them with honesty and integrity.

And on those days that you feel you cannot possibly serve another human being, be honest with yourself, and don't go out and serve. Take a look at how much time you spend trying to fulfill your own dreams and the requests of others. Keep that in balance . . . and sing!

I am a fan of tithing and giving, but remember that when you give it must come from your heart. If it cannot come from the heart, then it has selfish motives. It's better not to give when it takes too much of your energy and time. Look at the higher picture. What serves more people in this moment? Would it better serve others if you were out giving, or would it be better that you lie low and keep your resources to yourself at this time? Humility takes balance: it's not just about giving to others, it is about giving to yourself when the need arises, so that you can reserve your energy and resources in order to give to others in the future. I describe the quality of grace as being in the moment and perfectly at peace and humility as the action behind the grace, being humble."

You must pass your days in song.
Let your whole life be a song.
—SAI BABA

SIX

Youthful Passions

A song has a few rights the same as ordinary citizens . . .
if it happens to feel like flying where humans cannot fly . . .
to scale mountains that are not there, who shall stop it?

—Charles Ives

Music has always played a significant role in my passion for life. Music is everywhere. If we pay attention, we'll notice that music surrounds us at all times.

Think about it: you rarely see a movie or television program without some type of musical score playing in the background. Even when there's no music playing in the literal sense (radio, television, stereo, singing), if you pay attention to the environment around you, you'll hear music everywhere: the rain pounding on the roof outside the building, the hum of a fan in the background, the birds singing in the trees, the gurgle of the pipes in the sink.

Everything has its own music. We just choose to blend notes and artfully put words (poetry) to those notes. And then they become song.

When I was young, I was attracted to different types of music. I studied music theory in high school and continued some musical studies in college, though I didn't pursue intellectual music study. I was more interested in the aesthetics of music. I was especially passionate about the ways music can turn into song. In this chapter, I'm going to talk about my attraction to certain music and certain artists, and what these songs have meant to me.

THE CARPENTERS, CRYSTAL GAYLE, AND PATSY CLINE'S CRAZY—IMITATION

When I was a teenager, if I found a voice that was of a similar quality to my own, I could almost perfectly imitate the recording artist. Two of my favorite singers were Karen Carpenter and Crystal Gayle. Crystal had caught my attention because she was very delicate in her expression. I would watch her on television and want to mimic her actions as well as her voice. Not to mention the wonderful long hair that flowed down to touch the floor and was just as impressive as her song!

Karen Carpenter had a voice so similar to my own that people could not tell the difference. One afternoon I was the passenger in my father's vehicle. The song *We've Only Just Begun* was playing on the radio. I was singing along. We pulled into our driveway. My father shut off the car (and the radio) and I kept singing. Dad kept adjusting the radio knobs. Then he looked at me, noticed I was still singing and said, "Oh, I thought the radio was still on!"

I took it on as a greater challenge for me to imitate other

artists, and it became something of an obsession throughout my adolescence. I sat for hours, playing the records, singing the songs, and copying the voices, following something of the same technique used by Roger Tenney when he blended our high school voices: he said that if two voices are similarly matched, the choristers will begin to imitate one another.

I suppose that this is how some musical groups are so beautifully harmonized. Although singing different notes, they are singing in a blended way by matching (or imitating) the sound qualities of the person or persons with whom they are harmonizing.

> Country music is three chords and the truth.
>
> HARLAN HOWARD

When I was in my twenties, I used to like to sing Patsy Cline's *Crazy* at karaoke night. She's easy to copy as far as the basic song goes, but it's very difficult to reproduce the timbre that makes her voice unique. I practiced at home and then took my performance onto the stage at the local pub. I never quite obtained the perfection that I would have liked; in fact, my sister does a much better job with her music than I do. Patsy Cline is a legend, never to be replicated, but it's fun to try.

Here is my theory on the likes of the Patsy Cline, Elvis, Beethoven, Buddy Holly, John Denver, the music greats of our world whose lives were taken abruptly, people who lived short but inspirational lives: I believe that each lifetime has a sole (soul) purpose to fulfill. The aforementioned souls' lives were all about the music and the message. They lived it with every ounce of their consciousness during their short time on earth. They brought us great compositions, incredible songs, and amazing vocals that changed society. They are transformers in music who determined humanity's course throughout time . . . through music.

VISUALIZING DETAILS AND PERFECTING IMITATION

Although imitation is an action (matching your voice with another person's voice), it's not exactly a quality. But the satisfaction of being able to perfect your singing voice to meet that of a professional is worthy of a meditation/visualization.

It's important to pay attention to details in any type of successful endeavor. It's possible that the combination of this meditation and the pursuit of imitation with your voice may lead you to understand other things that may be relevant to your success.

It's been said that once a person masters a certain area of life, it is very easy to master another area, because the principles of making it to mastership are the same. The only difference is the specialized skill set needed to complete the various types of tasks/work. So learning to imitate a voice may help you gain understanding in another aspect of work, career, or life. The quality of imitation in the voice can help you examine details.

This visualization may seem irrelevant to singing. However, if you become "in charge" of the way you view things, that attention to detail can help you in all areas of life.

Whether or not you sing another's song is not the point of this visualization. The point is to bring you to a place where you can look for details in any aspect of your life. In this context it's used to imitate another person's vocals, but you can use it to help you do just about anything in your life that calls for a detailed examination.

Visualize: Sit quietly, take a deep breath, and release it. Imagine that there's a large bubble of light in front of you. Within this bubble of light you see other, smaller bubbles of light. Examine the big bubble of light. What do you see? It doesn't matter what you see, or what you experience from this large bubble of light: just observe. If you see nothing, that's fine; it's what you see.

Now observe the smaller bubbles of light inside the larger bubble of light. Notice that these smaller bubbles carry the same traits as the larger bubble. These details are smaller, because the bubble is smaller. Now go back and observe the large bubble of light and add something to this light—something like laughter or excitement or other aspects of light. You may tone down the light. You may add another color. You may add some texture. Whatever your imagination can dream up, add it to the larger bubble of light. And when you have, examine the smaller bubbles within the large bubble of light. Notice that it conforms to the larger bubble. It has a smaller density of the qualities you added to the larger bubble of light.

Now imagine that you're walking into the large bubble of light, and that you are surrounded by the smaller bubbles of light. If you can, imagine that you're *becoming* the same qualities in the large bubble of light, so that you blend with those temperaments that you added to it. You are becoming a part of the energy of the large bubble of light, yet you are individual in keeping your own consciousness and your own awareness of who you are within this bubble of light.

At this point, change something inside yourself, like adding a feeling, or recognizing how you are feeling. If you are feeling contentment, then bring this to your awareness and see the large bubble of light conforming to the contentment in your body. Now notice the smaller bubbles of light: they are also conforming to this contentment. Stay for a while in this larger bubble of light and play with it; see how it changes as you become aware of parts of your being and add them to the bubble. It also changes the smaller bubbles. This is how you can adapt to your environment, and adjust your environment to adapt to you and your needs.

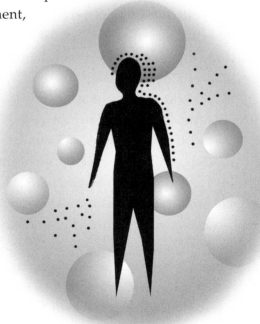

THE ROSE—LOVE

*When the power of love overcomes the love of power,
the world will know peace.*

—JIMI HENDRIX

The Rose, a song written by Amanda McBroom and performed by Bette Midler in the movie of the same title, has long been a favorite of mine, not only because it's performed in a lower key (and therefore fits my alto voice quite well!), but also because it's a song I can sing with great expression. Why? Because it says almost exactly what I feel about love.

It's not always possible for others to love us the same way we love them. It's not always practical, because we have different life-experiences and our souls are different. We perceive life differently. And although another person may love, he or she may not express the love in the way that you and I perceive as love.

When I give love to someone now, I don't have any expectations for that love to be returned to me in a way that I understand. This other person may love me just as much as I love him or her—or even more—but may not demonstrate it to me in a way that I can understand or accept.

Therefore love *can* seem like a river. It can wash right over you and drown you. It can be suffocating. Or it can cut right through you like a razor, leaving your soul drenched in its own blood.

Some people do not demonstrate love in a way that we see as healthy. Some people don't know how. Others are drowning in loneliness.

I've always been an advocate of expressing love. When you love someone, tell them! Sometimes it's not possible to tell a person directly, but it's always possible to show someone through action—or through the subtler means of prayer or sending positive thoughts.

It is even possible to sing a song and share love through the act of singing. That's why I love *The Rose.* It gives me the opportunity to share my affection with others by singing the song and telling them that yes, we may be afraid to show our love, but through this message I tell you that I love you.

I sang *The Rose* at my sister's wedding. Singing it was a frightening experience; as I was singing, though, I caught sight of my young adult children watching me from the back of the church, and I instantly felt the most awesome quality of love come over me. I relaxed and finished the song successfully. It was a tribute to the couple's love, and also a reminder that I need to keep my loved ones in my heart and always share the love that I feel with others. This can be done by sharing a song, by humming in the grocery store, by speaking one's words fluently, and by allowing music to be the expression of love that one gives to oneself and others in magical ways.

The Quality of Love

Love is a feeling, but it's also a quality, and that's how I use it in this book. The expression of love is something that you can develop, and all of the qualities mentioned in this book are aspects within yourself that can be integrated.

You can feel love for yourself and other people, for the

animals and the plants, and for the earth. You can feel love, and you can act on love. Love can grow, it can deepen, and it can build. Also, the more you identify with love in your heart, the more you will give to others from that love.

Others will be drawn to you increasingly because of that love. Love is an extremely versatile quality. Love can take many abuses and many hits, and it comes back standing. Love can be embellished by beautiful music. Romance can be had through the use of beautiful music. Passion can be inspired by listening to music. But the quality of love must be innate, and it must come from the heart. Use song and singing to accentuate the love in your heart. Share that love through song. *Sing, sing a song . . . sing of happy, not sad.*

SOMEWHERE IN THE LAND OF OZ— BEAUTY AND DREAMS

If you can dream it, you can do it.

—WALT DISNEY

Way, way back in time when I was a kid, *The Wizard of Oz* was shown once a year on network television. Usually it aired on a Sunday night at six o'clock. I remember the excitement growing every year on the weekend that *Oz* was going to be on.

(Today it's simply a matter of taking the movie, putting it in the machine and turning it on, but my generation could only see the show once a year. It became a family event.)

I was always fascinated by that story. I was particularly enthralled by Judy Garland singing *Over the Rainbow.* (I even psychoanalyzed Dorothy's dream and wrote a forty-page paper on it for a psychology class in college. I was obsessed with Oz for a long time!) I imagined myself floating way up high, over the clouds, beyond the rainbow. What could be found out there so far away? Blue skies, happiness, anything could come true, all of our dreams happening as fast as we could dream them.

What if troubles would melt away like lemon drops? Imagine the lemony taste of stress relief! I watched the little munchkins dancing about and imagined a life as bright and colorful as Oz (for even though we watched it on a black-and-white television, the colors were vivid in my mind's eye). I painted a picture in my head and I sang lively songs. I fantasized that the wicked witch was coming to get me, but then the good witch came to save me. I saw Oz as bigger than life, sending me home where I arrived to the cheers of all my friends and family. Somewhere over the rainbow was the place to make my dreams come true. I still use this scenario today.

Visualizing Beauty and Dreams: If you want to play music during this visualization, make sure it is lively and fun. Sit quietly, close your eyes; take a deep breath, and release it. Imagine yourself as a young child between the ages of six and twelve. As this child, you are running through a field, on the beach . . . anywhere that makes you feel free and delighted. Imagine yourself in this place, twirling and running and jumping and playing with all of the free-spiritedness that you can muster.

Experience the feeling of being free. Imagine the song from the heavens. What does it sound like? Where does it come from? How do you make it happen; how do you feel this freedom? You have no attachments and no obligations. You feel as though the wind can lift you and carry you to new heights. Feel that freedom in your body.

Begin to see an energy field around your body filled with a beautiful white light that permeates through your body and carries you like a ball of white light wherever you want to go in the Universe. Feel this lightness, this freedom in your body. Begin to breathe the freedom that you feel. As you hear the heavenly music playing, open up your hearing. Hear each note, how it's played, and what sensation it brings to your body. You are free. You are love. You can create anything you wish in this space of freedom. Visualize your most important dreams coming true, and what they would look like. When you're finished, open your eyes and continue that feeling of love throughout your day.

SEVEN

Traveling Tunes

> Music is the mediator between the spiritual
> and the sensual life.
>
> —LUDWIG VAN BEETHOVEN

I have many stories of being on the road in search of good music. I will travel a long distance for a dose of good music. In these next stories, I tell about important experiences I've had involving the music I love, and the lengths to which I will go to get my share.

SISTERS IN NASHVILLE—ACCOMPLISHMENT AND RESPECT

The story of song in my life wouldn't be complete without sharing a few memories that involve my sister Sarah. We're six years apart in age, but nonetheless were often coupled together in song by our parents. I remember us singing *It's a Small World* as a duet for friend audiences on occasion—and one time even onstage at a family function. How embarrassed I used to feel! I knew that my sister could sing well, but I did not feel confident about my own voice, ever. Sarah seemed to have incredible poise onstage; I was just the opposite. In performance mode I always felt like I needed to escape my body. I became light-headed and almost faint. Once the performance began, though, I'd usually feel better.

My sister, Sarah Ennis Zak, has performed as a vocalist at many different venues, including as lead singer for several bands, and at contests, weddings, funerals, etc. I consider her a semi-professional singer. I asked Sarah how it is that she always looks so confident up there onstage. She told me that since it's not always appropriate to take a drink, especially when singing at a funeral (we laughed) she often prays before performances.

Sarah sang *the Lord's Prayer* at our maternal grandmother's funeral. We both loved our grandmother very much; she'd cared for us whenever our mother was away and became our second mother. I knew that singing such a beautiful song in tribute to a woman she loved so much would be very hard for Sarah, but oh, my! How incredible was this moment! She had me in tears by the time she finished, and yet she herself did not crack on a single note. She broke down afterward, for sure, but she maintained her composure through the entire piece. Wow! I was impressed. The day she asked me to sing at her wedding, however, I freaked. "I can't do that. I can't sing in public."

"Yes, you can and you will," she responded. I couldn't get out of that one, so I did sing at her wedding.

Sarah says that "singing a duet is easier for me than singing solo." She "likes singing with other people, the togetherness of it." Harmonies can be difficult, though she explains, "either I can do it or I can't. I have to be able to hear myself and the harmony I'm singing, or I can't do it." There are some vocalists with whom it's hard to harmonize because of their vocal quality and output. It's a matter of blending. "With some people it's easy to blend and with others, not so easy," she explains, but Sarah encourages everyone to sing. "Just to sing and enjoy music. It's good for the soul."

One of the most unforgettable adventures of my life is the trip that Sarah and I took to Nashville, Tennessee. Sarah's a lifelong fan of country music. I loved country music as a child, but neglected to listen to it for many years during early adulthood, only to pick up my respect for it again in the last fifteen years or so. In 1996 my husband and I moved to Nashville for two years, and found of course that music is the mainstay of life in Nashville. I was reintroduced to a new love for the twang and the savvy of country.

In 2001, Sarah and I took off from our hometown in Minnesota, bound for Music City. Sarah had written some music and wanted to get a feel for the songwriting industry.

On the first day, we just did some sightseeing. On the second day we watched as country artists walked down the red carpet to open the new Country Music Hall of Fame in downtown Nashville. The crowds were outrageous, so Sarah and I chose to walk away and view the sights from afar. As we stood at a crosswalk, waiting for the light to change, a procession of limousines and country music star carriages lined up in front of us. The car across from us was a convertible with the top down. It was about fifty feet away from us so we could not make out who it was in the back seat, but whoever it was kept staring right at us. I commented to Sarah, "She's staring at us."

"I know. Who is she?" We walked closer, daring to cross the street behind the vehicle. As we approached, the vehicle moved forward. It was Trisha Yearwood! I whispered, "It's Trisha Yearwood . . . I *love* Trisha!"

Sarah was just as excited. "I know. I know. I love her, too! And she's been staring at us!" What an ego trip that was for both of us!

As her car pulled away, we blew kisses her way and I shouted (as respectfully as one can shout), "We love you, Trisha!" and she yelled, "Thank you!" from the back seat. This absolutely made my day!

Meeting Ms. Yearwood this way was a delight. The first time I ever heard her perform was as a backup singer for Garth Brooks. I was watching the performance on a thirteen-inch television, but even through that small lens, I could see the gentleness of her personality. I saw her care and compassion radiate and when I heard her voice, her grace was articulated in song. There is a quality within Trisha's personality that compels people to listen; when they do and they hear that voice, they are mesmerized and enchanted. She's a beautiful music goddess who gives us great gifts through her art.

On the last day of our Nashville vacation, Sarah and I walked down Music Row. We even walked into an office or two to get the feel for the big time. We had a meeting with a record producer who told us what to do to get a hit record in the industry. And on our last night in the Music City we went to Tootsie's Orchid Lounge.

It was our hope that we could persuade the folks at Tootsie's to allow Sarah to sing with the house band, which she did. She sang two songs, and sounded as if she'd been in the music scene all her life. The audience went nuts and I, of course, was very proud of her. She sounded terrific, and her show was fantastic.

Sarah says that auditions are scary for her. I sense that she'd rather just perform in the show and forget the audition. She also suffers from migraine headaches, and says that if she has one before a gig or performance it often goes away once she is singing for the audience. So you might say that singing is the perfect medicine!

Everyone can sing, at least to some extent. In fact, what does it hurt to sing in the shower? Or in the car, alone? Music is to be felt and expressed. Sarah has even offered to help me "get people to sing." Once you let it out and sing to your heart's content, you could feel a newfound sense of accomplishment and respect for yourself, one that you've never felt before.

QUALITIES OF ACCOMPLISHMENT AND RESPECT

It is important to feel accomplished at something in life, and have respect for that accomplishment. Singing a song is a simple way to do that. This visualization, aims to create a sense of accomplishment. If you do this technique often enough, and you play the music that makes you feel accomplished, then you will begin to sense accomplishment and respect every day in your life.

Visualization: Begin by sitting quietly; take a deep breath, and release it. Imagine your heart in the center of your chest; fill your heart with a rose-colored light. Light is coming in on all sides of you and filling up the center of your chest, the cavity around your heart, with a rose-colored light. You may even smell roses. You may wish to burn a rose-scented candle to help!

As your chest cavity begins to fill up with rose-colored light, begin to see your heart beaming with great intensity. You can see your heart pulse this rose-colored light, and as it does, the waves of the rose light go out in all directions from you. You begin to feel very certain of your life path, and very successful at what you have done so far. In your imagination (or in actuality) pat yourself on the back, for you have done what you set out to do!

Respect yourself with this heart light. Tell yourself that you deserve to have what you want in life. Bring more of the rose-colored light into your heart area. Fill your entire body with the rose-colored light, so that when you acknowledge other people in your life, at least in terms of the imagination, they see only the rose-colored light when they look at you, and they feel your success, your accomplishment.

You can add music to this meditation. Whenever you hear a song that makes you feel proud, stop for a moment and see the rose-colored heart light pulsating in your body and radiating outward. Then, begin to sing the music with a proud voice, as if you were in front of ten people, one hundred people, one thousand people and then tens of thousands of people in a stadium. You are the main attraction at this moment, and you are doing well.

See it, own it, feel good about it, and have fun with it.

When the song is over, come back to life and start from there. The more you honor yourself in any way, the better you will begin to feel about yourself; this feeling will carry over into your daily life in ways that will give you little successes that become bigger with time and effort. Have fun with this, but remember that it takes time to build a life from visualization—and patience is a virtue.

TUNING IT UP IN TELLURIDE—WAY UP

I love concerts, especially those in open-air venues like Red Rocks Amphitheater near Golden, Colorado, or—in this case—the Telluride Bluegrass Festival, held every year in June in the beautiful mountain town of Telluride, Colorado.

In the summer of 1993 I was able to attend the festival. It was such a novelty for me that I even forgot my tickets to the event. In my excitement I invited a girlfriend from Minnesota to attend with me, picked her up at the airport (I lived in Boulder, Colorado, at the time), drove into the mountains to the festival, only to discover at the admissions desk that I had no tickets. Emmylou Harris was on stage in fifteen minutes. My favorite bluegrass entertainer of all time, the reason

I bought the tickets in the first place, was about to be on stage. And I had no tickets! They were on the dresser back at home.

So what could I do? I convinced the ticket agent to let us in, based on the promise that my tickets would be arriving via airmail in the morning. What a fabulous concert it was. Emmylou rocked the house, my tickets came the next morning, and we spent the weekend in bluegrass bliss.

The next day was filled with fabulous entertainment. Being from a small town in the Midwest, I had never experienced a concert in the mountains like this. The weather in Telluride in June is cool, and hot, and rainy, and fabulous. We spent all day at the festival. In the morning it was cool enough for jackets and sweaters. Early afternoon we had stripped down to shorts and a shirt. By late afternoon we were covering ourselves with garbage bags to stay dry from the afternoon rain, all the while listening to fantastic bluegrass music.

Then came evening. Beautiful clear blue skies, glistening rainbows, and a sun retreating into the western mountains. Loreena McKennit came on stage with her massive harp. What a sensation! She began to play her music with such grace. My girlfriend and I stood within feet of the stage, in awe. Her long red hair and black gown went well with her music. The harp and her voice? . . . Oh, my, what radiance against the colored sky. It echoed off the four corners of the mountains. We could hear the sound of her angelic voice with harp backing her up coming at us from all directions. It was as if we'd been absorbed into the heavens and transported to a world we knew little about.

We were certainly captivated by the entertainment, and I was incredibly moved by the experience, taken to a place in my heart that I have yet to explain. The music in that environment changed me forever. I doubt I'll ever go back to the festival, mostly because I don't have to. I wouldn't want to change the memory of that experience by trying to redo it. This one I think is better left alone.

It was during this weekend at Telluride that I met someone who altered my life forever as well. This person told me that if I set my mind to it, I could do absolutely anything. He had only just met me, yet he told me this as if he had known me for years. It was exactly what I needed to hear, and I keep these words close to me always.

Indeed, the inspiration of the music in the mountains and the sage advice from a stranger are part of what keeps me on my mission to succeed in this life. I don't give up any more because of it. Tuning it *way up* in Telluride is the boost I needed in an unusual time in my life. This experience transformed my life forever.

ROCKY MOUNTAIN HIGH—TRIBUTE TO SPIRIT

> Music gives a soul to the universe, wings to the mind,
> flight to the imagination, and life to everything.
>
> —PLATO

John Denver. What a superb songwriter and musician. I guess I was somewhat a typical teenager of the seventies, although I did not participate in the drugs or the hardcore rock-and-roll, as did many of my peers. But I loved John

Denver's music and became somewhat obsessed with him, as many teens do regarding music idols.

Even though I was mostly a loner, I had three very close female friends in high school. We did everything together. We studied together, we went shopping together, and we went cruising together. We also went to see John Denver in concert. My friend Teri invited an older guy, a high school graduate, to go with us and drive us to the concert. I was already a John Denver groupie: in junior high, my physical education teacher was the sister of Annie, John's first wife, for whom he wrote *Annie's Song.*

The evening of the concert, I couldn't think of anything besides going backstage where I could be closer to Mr. Denver. Indeed, with a bit of crafty maneuvering, my friend Michelle and I made it to the backstage area and stood only ten feet from John while he sang *Rocky Mountain High.* My head was certainly in the clouds for a very long time after that!

It was always my dream to meet this man in person, but my memories will have to do, as John Denver is no longer with us in this dimension. I imagine that he soars with the eagles in spirit, writing music from another vantage point.

John's music brought me home. When I was twelve years old I went on a very fast vacation with family to the Rocky Mountains. We spent one day in the mountains and then came back home to the Midwest. I remember how awed I felt that day in the mountains. The feeling of ecstasy was significant. I had never experienced such greatness in my life. I had never been much away from home. I never knew that geography could create such magnitude of feeling within me.

I did not return to the mountains until my early thirties. It was then that I could actually relate to the song *Rocky Mountain High. He was born in the summer of his twenty-seventh year, coming home to a place he'd never been before.* This was exactly how I felt when I was in the mountains that day when I was twelve.

I remember calling my father collect from a pay phone in a small mountain town. He asked, "Are you having fun?"

I said, "Oh, Dad, you would not believe how beautiful it is here! They have houses in the mountains, and they're so high. And it feels so good here!"

It was in my thirty-second year that I decided to treat myself to a birthday gift. I went alone to Colorado to visit the Rockies from a more mature perspective. I wanted to see if what I felt when I was twelve on that quick visit to the mountains was correct.

It was. I certainly felt the Rocky Mountain high and it wasn't just the altitude. It was the magnitude of the landscape.

Since that time I have lived in various locations in the Rocky Mountains. I have chosen to live outside of that region at this time for work reasons, but I will go back someday soon. I cannot seem to get my work done in the mountains just yet. Someday my budget will afford both my creative work and a life in the mountains.

Now he walks in quiet solitude the forest and the streams, seeking grace in every step he takes. It was in Boulder, Colorado, that I realized how deeply in love I am with our planet. I was alone, after many years of marriage and of being a wife and a mother. I was no longer living with my family. My heart, although hurting deeply, was contented by the fact that it is so beautiful in the mountains.

One day when I was feeling sorry for myself I went for a hike into the foothills. I was crying to my Maker that I did not understand why life had taken such a wrong turn for me. At that moment, I looked over to my left and saw a gigantic rock. Behind it was a magnificent foothill of the Rockies. I walked over to the boulder and leaned against it. Right then I knew that the Earth had been sculpted for our enjoyment. I always see beauty in all of the landscapes. There is beauty in the mountains, beauty in the desert, austerity in the greenery of the Midwest, and a reverence to behold at the ocean's edge. I can even see the glory in artificial environments, like the big city.

But I prefer the Rocky Mountain High.

It is in my heart to live on a mountain peak and I nourish that wish every day. I say to myself, every day, that someday when the time is right I will live in the mountains, and I will truly appreciate the asceticism and gifts of that landscape. But I realize that not until I have full appreciation for this life I've been given will I have the opportunity to return home again.

One thing that has my heart aching is made clear by a verse in John Denver's music: *Now his life is full of wonder, but his heart still knows some fear of a simple thing he cannot comprehend: why they try to tear the mountains down to bring in a couple more. More people, more scars upon the land.* It saddens my heart to watch the development in and around the mountains, and in other parts of the untapped countryside. Certainly people deserve to have a nice home in which to live, in a beautiful location, and shopping establishments. But it's ruining our landscapes.

We must find answers to this, for I am certain that what breaks my heart is also what tore John Denver's heart apart as well. The man was ahead of his time. He had a great need to see beauty and to express it to others. He did this with his music. Many artists have given us just such gifts through music. John sang the song and told us to be careful. "Don't destroy the land," is what I imagine he would say today. "Do not kill one another with greed and ambition."

Rocky Mountain High is the way for me to remember my purpose as a human being and my dreams as a member of society.

A Tribute to Spirit—As the Eagle Flies

Close your eyes. Sit quietly. Take a deep breath, and release it. Imagine that you are sitting on top of a mountain. On all sides you see the valley. And from what seems to be the "heavens" you hear a grand orchestra playing.

As you are sitting on this mountain peak, you see a lone eagle flying off in the distance. The eagle swoops in front of you, goes back up in the air. You see it climb almost to the point that you can no longer keep it in sight. You watch the eagle circle and see it glide with the wind currents through the air. Soon you see another eagle off in the distance. Now there are two.

The first eagle takes a dive into the valley, coming back up, interacting with the second eagle in flight. The second eagle then takes a lunge into the valley and moves back upward. The two eagles are in a dance with one another. The music becomes louder and more extreme. You feel the percussion section of the orchestra very intensely at this point. A crescendo is happening with the music, and suddenly you begin to sing from the mountaintop.

It is not important that you understand the language in which you are singing. All that matters is that your voice is resounding throughout the valley at an awesome pitch, in alignment with a choir of angels singing from the heavens. You have entered into spirit energy with the earth, the animals, the music, and the heavens. Your voice is an angel's voice singing with the music. Your voice encourages the eagles to dance even more eloquently. Your voice makes the sunshine more positive. Your voice encourages the earth to continue to support it. And your voice allows the heavenly voice its place here on earth. Continue to sing, sending your intentions out to the earth and into the heavens for healing.

Memory at Mingus

It was on top of Mingus Mountain in Prescott National Forest, Arizona, that I first saw eagles in flight, doing that dance. What awesome beauty! My husband and I parked our rickety old RV at the top of the mount and sat out on the cliffs each day to watch the eagle dance and wait for the thousands of bats to come out of the caves inside the cliffs. An amazing switch from one to the other. We climbed into the RV at just about dusk, before the bats appeared. We listened to music on the CD player and watched the sky become dark with the flight of the night animals.

I have yet to know what songs could be written from this experience.

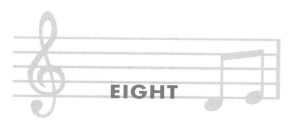

EIGHT

Nature's Song

All the sounds of the earth are like music.

—Oscar Hammerstein

[n all of nature there is song. For instance, last night as I was falling asleep, I heard the yowl of a coyote, which set off all the dogs in the neighborhood. So we had a choir of animals to put us to sleep!

The birds in the spring are often so enthusiastic about new growth and adventures with nesting that the air is filled with beautiful variations of coos and crackles. If you live outside of the city at all, often there will be animal and nature sounds that alert your rhythmic senses, perhaps keeping beat with the earth's pulse.

In the South we have the cicada bugs in the summertime that whistle their high-pitched chatter. We have trees falling in the woods at times that create big booms at unexpected moments, so the rhythm of the forest is not consistent. The tree frogs definitely keep me awake at night. It's fun to listen to nature sounds just before a storm. We can tell when it is just about time for the rain to fall because the animal voices stop, and a deep silence comes over the forest. The tree frogs stop their incessant croaking. That deep, guttural, echoing song of the frogs ceases only for the time that it is raining, and the moment the rain quits, the frog concerto resumes.

In the city there are other sounds that are equivalent to nature sounds: cars, alarms, sirens, and people talking and yelling. All environmental noises can be musical at times. We've all been sitting in a waiting area and have been tapping our fingers or shaking our foot to the beat, keeping pace with the existential tempo of the Universe. Or find ourselves humming while standing in line or in the shower.

Often we hear music played in shopping malls, doctor's offices, or out on the streets. When I was young (and even to this day) Christmas music was piped through the downtown area of the town in which I grew up. It is lovely to walk the streets with snowflakes falling, listening to the music floating through the air. It's impossible not to sing along and get caught up in the ambiance of the holiday spirit, regardless of one's religion. The energy of music, the vibration of spirit is contagious. In my opinion, adding music to nature's already irresistible sound just adds to the pleasurable sensation. Add to that shopping for gifts for loved ones, and the "package" is complete. Music is the icing on the cake! Nature creates music.

O BEAUTIFUL

National Anthems. Most countries in the world (and even individual states, cities, towns and institutions) have anthems, theme songs that describe the essence of the particular territory or landscape and her people. The lyrics of the US national anthem were written by Francis Scott Key in 1814. Although the *Star-Spangled Banner* references the American flag, as it represents the *home of the brave* and the *land of the free,* in the second verse we sing about the flag as it flies above its people, as in the fight for the land. *Now it catches the gleam of the morning's first beam. In full glory reflected, now shines on the stream.*

Some groups of Americans, however, have from time to time strongly advocated that we change our national anthem to *America the Beautiful,* as they feel it better describes the nation in which we live, and its landscape. Also, they stress that it's easier to sing. The *Star-Spangled Banner* has a range of an octave and a half, which is difficult for most people to sing.

The lyrics for *America the Beautiful* were written in 1893 by Katharine Lee Bates. She was an English teacher at Wellesley College and was traveling from the east coast to Colorado when she wrote the poem. Later the music was added, taken from a hymn composed by Samuel A. Ward (Materna). *Oh beautiful for spacious skies, for amber waves of grain, for purple mountain majesty, above the fruited plain! . . . from sea to shining sea.* Ms. Bates wanted to bring about the respect and honor to the heroes that saved this land. The latter verses describe that victory. *America the Beautiful* is on my singing favorites list for sure!

I have chosen to examine several other national anthems as a part of nature's song. I'm not playing favorites with countries, but in view of the numbers involved, I couldn't examine them all! I chose three: Austria (because my dear friend lives there and I will be visiting soon), Canada, and Mexico (because we share the same continent).

I feel, as I've stated earlier, that we need to become one worldwide country, keeping our individual identities as nations, but unifying our thoughts, ideals, and certainly our music. I'd love to have time to examine each nation's anthem, learn the languages of those anthems, and sing them all over the world. I do believe that dreams come true, but this is a lofty one and will take some time and diligence on my part. Someday I'm sure I'll dig into it.

I've chosen these three anthems for personal reasons, but also to examine them for proof that anthems do often refer to nature and the landscape of the countries they represent.

The Austrian national anthem is titled *Land der Berge, Land am Strome* (land of mountains, land on the stream). There is some confusion about the actual composer of the music, of the melody, for this anthem. It used to be thought that Wolfgang Amadeus Mozart was the creator of the piece (from *Freimaurerkantate*, KV 623), but now it is more widely known that it was an acquaintance of his, Johann Holzer, who actually documented the composition.

(In any case, my research has swelled an urge within me to lose myself in classical music once again. I left it long ago to delve into other types of music, but I have such appreciation for the elegance and depth of the classical.)

The Austrian national anthem is riddled with landscape references: land of fields, land of cathedrals, a people blessed by their sense of beauty.

Most anthems speak of how courageous the people are

and the freedoms they will have and the beauty that is found in the land.

The Canadian national anthem is *Oh, Canada.* Its melody was written by Calixa Lavallee in 1880 with lyrics by Sir Adolphe Basile Routhier, also in 1880. It was written originally in French with the English translation (by Robert Stanley Weir) completed in 1908. The anthem does not directly depict the landscape but rather states its desire for protection of the land. *We stand on guard for thee. God keep our land glorious and free.* The song shows a love for the land and the sacredness of the land that her people are protecting.

The Mexican national anthem is titled *Himno Nacional Mexicano* and is a bit more laden with war images. The national hymn does, however, make reference to the beautiful land, the *mountains and valleys,* the *olive wreathes,* the nation's children that defend and protect, but also shows the strength, the resolve of the people to keep the country safe and within their own possession.

We all have our homelands that we want and need to protect. This discourse regarding national anthems and/or hymns written for national protection could go on endlessly. My purpose in this is to point out that there are many songs written about nature, geography, animals and people in all languages everywhere.

> America! America! God shed his grace on thee,
> And crown thy good with brotherhood,
> from sea to shining sea!

What a beautiful land we all live in—and not just those of

us in the United States. We all have a land to protect and honor. By singing songs in tribute we show her our respect, and feel her beauty deep in our hearts.

> Land of Heart's Desire, Where beauty has no ebb, decay, no flood. But joy is wisdom, time an endless song.
> —WILLIAM BUTLER YEATS

THE FOUR ELEMENTS—EARTH, WIND, WATER, FIRE

In tribute to our beautiful planet I would like to address songs that relate to the four elements, earth, wind, water and fire.

Earth Song

Recently as I was driving I heard the song *Try to Remember* with its references to the days of September. I remembered the song and related it to when I was a youngster. I loved having my birthday parties in early September. It was still warm, the leaves were starting to turn bright colors, and this song was playing on the radio. It has a laid-back sound and even mentions how mellow life was back in September. Ah, my favorite time of year.

I can hardly talk about earth songs without mentioning native tribal American music. The traditional music is kept alive by many dancers and musicians. It was always exciting every summer when my family and I took our annual vacation up in the northern Land of Ten Thousand Lakes. I swear it's true, Minnesota does have ten thousand lakes, and it seems like my family and I have fished most of them! Many of the lakes we stayed at were near the Indian reservations.

Pow-wows were frequently held for tourists in the small towns nearby. I was quite taken by the music, the drumming, the chanting, and especially the dance. I loved the dance, both watching and participating, as the younger members would pull in some of the children from the audience.

I always felt as if I belonged, somehow, as if I'd done this routine many times in a past life. I could even recite the chant perfectly. It made me feel so alive and close to our Mother Earth. The music relates to my soul. There is so much music and so many teachings from these traditions, from all traditions for that matter, that I am unable to get started even in this book. I am just relaying to you my experiences.

In 1995 Michael Jackson released a CD single entitled *Earth Song*. It became the number-one Christmas song on the charts in the United Kingdom that year. Mr. Jackson describes the horrors of things that are happening here on the earth, the rain forests being destroyed by loggers, animals being killed by poachers, wars destroying people's homes in many places across the planet. The video depicts how horrendously brutal our world is today, and at the end shows everything magically returning to a beautiful and peaceful land and us living as one people.

This song has become one of my favorite "mood" songs. I play songs like this whenever I feel that I need strength to move forward in my public work and to get through rough patches in my personal life. There are many gifted songwriters who have the heartbeat of the world within their own souls, and we're blessed when they write about it, as did Michael Jackson.

Earth Meditation

A great way to connect yourself physically with the earth, in times when you are feeling lost, emotionally distraught, or even flighty (can't bring your thoughts together) and be a part of this daily earth walk, is to gather your favorite music on a headset or MP3. Pick music that is a part of the moment you are in. Put on your headphones and go outside and walk. It doesn't matter where you walk, just so long as you have earth beneath your feet.

With the first step you take, imagine that your own personal energy is going into the earth with your foot. With the next step, imagine that the earth's energy is coming up through your foot, up through your body and circulating into the next footstep. Your energy goes down and comes up through the next foot (changing the order of energy direction every so often.) In each set of steps that you take, you interact with the earth.

You can imagine light going through your body into the earth and coming back up from the earth to your body. Just connect strongly with the earth. Imagine that you are one with the earth, and the music you are listening to is also connecting with the earth song with each step you take. All you need to walk is five to ten minutes in this manner and I assure you will feel more connected to the planet that gives you life and a home than you did before you began the walk.

Wayward Wind Song

There are many songs written about the wind. I will mention a couple of my favorites and how music to me is in the wind itself. The wind plays a song with varying degrees of intensity. It has a density to it, a lightness to it, a movement and rhythm that come together and make a beautiful song. The music it produces can be cheerful or eerie, depending upon the strength, its velocity, and the heaviness of the current at the time.

Many years ago I was exposed to a lot of old country cowboy music, which I still love today. A classic wind song is *Wayward Wind.* This song tells us that the wind was restless just like the cowboy singing it. He promises his woman he'll stay forever, but cannot keep that promise . . . as he is like the wind and yearns to wander. Songs tell a story, and this song compares the element of restless wind to the cowboy's character.

My personal "wind" story: When I was between six and ten years old, I used to love to dress up in my mother's old gowns, such as her prom and homecoming dresses. My sister and I would gather the gowns and pretend to be princesses. One windy afternoon, I was outside wearing a beautiful gown with lots of petticoats and ruffles. I was quite small at the time so the dress was huge. Nonetheless I was able to gather the dress about me and twirl around and sing my songs of royalty, when all of a sudden a wind gust came up underneath the dress, picked me up and carried me several feet. Wow! I was so thrilled. For a long time after that I thought I could recreate the situation, so I put on the dress (on a windy day of course), head outside, began to twirl and sing the same song.

It never happened again, but I will always remember the feeling of being lifted away by the wind-song.

The actual *Wind Song* was written by John Denver. In this song Mr. Denver writes about how the wind is the whisper of our Mother Earth, and how it can bring bad and good tidings. He relates the wind to that which connects all of nature and asks us to listen to the wisdom that the wind offers us, to let the wind surround us and then lift up our voices and sing with the wind.

A Wind Visualization: Close your eyes. Imagine that you are standing in the middle of a very large open space. It could be a field of daisies, sunflowers, or wheat; or you might be on the beach by a lake or the ocean, or standing on the mountaintop. But you are standing in a large clearing. It is very quiet, when suddenly you feel a slight breeze come across your face and your body. It feels good. It is as if the wind is speaking to you, so you begin to listen more closely. The wind picks up speed and is blowing your hair and your clothing. You might feel a bit of sand or dust blowing across your body. The wind is telling you something in this moment as well. What is the wind telling you?

Now the wind begins to swirl around you and becomes quite vicious. You hang on to the nearest tree or rock so that you are not blown about by the wind. It becomes a ferocious wind, yet it tells you something again. And then, just as rapidly as it picked up speed, the wind quiets to nothing but a soft breeze. Ask the wind what it would like to tell you in this moment.

Water and Emotion

When I think of water as an element, I compare it to emotion in humans. Water can represent sadness, fulfillment, joy, or love (as in *My Cup Runneth Over*). Any emotion that has a fluid, liquid feeling to it can be represented symbolically by water.

Some classical music can be very liquid and emotional. The two songs referring to water that I like are *Michael, Row the Boat Ashore* and *Bridge Over Troubled Water*.

Michael, Row the Boat Ashore is an old African-American spiritual that predates the Civil War. It is often sung these days as a lullaby, but actually was used as a singing prayer to the archangel Michael helping the slaves cross over the Jordan safely. Another row-the-boat song (*Row, Row, Row Your Boat*) is sung usually in a round, a musical composition for two or more voices, often large groups split into two or more smaller groups. These groups sing the same melody, but begin the song at different times.

Bridge Over Troubled Water is a beautiful song to sing, yet it seems to have a range that I find difficult to cover. The song however, makes me feel compassionate and strong when I sing or listen. It describes friendship at its ultimate. *I will lay me down*, seems to say that no matter what, if you need me, I'll be there. I am drawn to songs that have interconnected-ness to other people and the spiritual side at the heart.

Of course we all know that songs can lead to different emotions. Studies have tested people who were feeling very optimistic and positive, and when songs were played that were instrumental alone, the positive mood would keep going.

Lyrics, however, often will change the mood in individuals. And in these studies, when lyrics were played that represented more depressed emotions, like sadness or hopelessness, the lyrics did seem to influence the mood in those who were already depressed (sometimes these songs helped to shift out the depression) and brought down the folk who were optimistic before the song was played.

There are many songs about love and emotion. Find your favorite songs and play the appropriate ones when you are feeling down and others when you want to further boost an upbeat moment. Better yet, sing along! Music has so much emotional influence over us.

Elevator music is soft, light, and upbeat. I've heard that it was originally chosen to prevent people from feeling panicked in the elevator. It promotes a satisfactory, pleasant experience when traveling in a confined space. Another word for this kind of music is *ambient*. Much of ambient music is composed electronically. It can be jazzy, new age, popular rock and roll, classical—in other words, any type of music that is soothing. This music can even be blocked out of awareness because it is played so softly in the background in many different places.

Some artists use animal and nature sounds to make their ambient music. Pay attention to all the places where ambient music is used: on the phone, in airports, restaurants, elevators, waiting rooms. Erik Satie first coined the term "furniture music" in the early 1920s: the music that the furniture will listen to. It is designed to play in the background, perhaps at a dinner party. Not music that you would intently put your ear to, but something that lends a mild flavor to the evening; this is one of the ways that background music came to be used. Artists, of course have taken off with that sound since then.

Some of the ambient music today could be considered techno music, and yet many artists from this genre have moved more into spiritually influenced new-age music, which uses a lot of natural sounds and rhythms within it to create a wholesome feeling. This is what I call water music, that which creates a feeling of calm, relaxation or love within the body.

Fire (Sun)

Throwing Fire at the Sun, by Helen Nova, talks about the fact that we have much depth within our souls and that everything is connected. I am also reminded of the phoenix, the mythological bird that is thrown into the fire and yet is reborn and comes out of the flame to fly again.

Or we can consider the spitfire phrase that speaks of love as burning. The song *Ring of Fire* was written in 1962 by June Carter and Merle Kilgore and included in the 2005 movie *Walk the Line.* In the movie, actor Reese Witherspoon used her own voice to sing as her character June Carter Cash. It has been said that she found the experience of singing in performance "horrifying."

There are many actors who sing as well as act. But for those who are asked to do a singing part when they've never done one before, it can be quite intense. It can be a "ring of fire" for sure!

All deep things are song.
It seems somehow the very central essence of us, song;
as if all the rest were but wrap pages and hulls.

—THOMAS CARLYLE

NINE

The Power of Music

Music was my refuge. I could crawl into the space
between the notes and curl my back to loneliness.

Maya Angelou

All throughout this book I've discussed how music influences our lives, and now I'd like to explore that notion a little more in depth. We often underestimate the power that music has over us, and if we are not aware of our complete surroundings and how they influence our day-to-day thinking, moods, and actions, then we cannot be whole.

Look around the environments in which you spend a lot of your time. How much music are you exposed to, and what types (not just actual music compositions, but sounds) are you hearing on a daily basis? Take a look at appendix A: *The Music Journal*. This will help you become aware.

Instead of robotically accepting your environment as it is and the exposure to music as it already exists in your life, I propose (as a counselor and firm believer in the power of positive creation) that you can change your mood, your comfort levels, the way you perceive reality and ultimately change what you bring into your life by being conscious about the music and sounds that are in your life.

Whereas in most work environments you cannot change either the music that is played or the sounds created around you, in your private environments, in your car or at home, you can pick and choose the music to which you expose yourself.

What I'm suggesting here is that we can change and enhance our lives by being more selective about the music and environmental noises we allow into our personal time and space. And we can also enjoy the process of vocalizing in song. Music has power.

> Music produces a kind of pleasure
> which human nature cannot do without.
>
> —CONFUCIUS

MUSIC AND HEALTH

Music is a vibration. The human body vibrates (oscillates). It makes sense that if a certain composition puts out a higher vibration than what the body is putting out, the body might try to emulate it and thus vibrate at a higher level. This could heal depression, fatigue, illness . . . the list goes on. And the benefits of singing can top even that!

In a study done and published by the National Library of Medicine on the benefits of singing for health, the survey of choral members revealed that over forty percent of respondents strongly agreed that singing helps improve mood, making them feel a lot happier. A principle components analysis identified six dimensions of benefits associated with singing. These were labeled as: benefits for well-being and relaxation, benefits for breathing and posture, social benefits, spiritual benefits, emotional benefits, and benefits for heart and immune system.

Playing music during simple medical procedures has been shown to relax patients. It is also thought that if a patient is listening to music, it makes for more suitable preparation for surgery. No studies have guaranteed the effects of music on patients while they are in surgery, but certainly the music enhances the pleasure factor for surgeons and operating room professionals. This is just one example of how music has power over our lives. Our health and well-being depend on it.

In the inner ear, the cochlea is what receives sound waves from the environment after coming through the outer ear and it tells our senses that there is movement. In the fetus of only twenty-two to twenty-six weeks, the function of the cochlea is almost matured. The functioning of the human ear is developed before the child is born. We are very auditory beings. Music can soothe babies and adults alike. From very early on in our development, hearing plays an important role in our daily life. Music can be used to enhance our world before we even enter into it.

VIBRATION

Music is a vibration. If you take a single note it would resonate at one vibration. You move to the next note and it resonates at another vibration. This goes into your hearing mechanism and for the most part it determines, according to the resonance of vibration, which notes are playing. We can tell when two notes sound good together or when they fight each other. We can hear a conglomeration of notes, a grouping of vibrations, and it can sound as if one note is playing. On an instrument, we can hear one, two, three, six notes or more playing at one time and sometimes it can sound like one note.

When people sing a solo (except for experienced throat singers, singing chords in one voice), they sing one note at a time. Therefore, in duets or quartets or choruses, several notes will be sung at the same time. Even different lyrics can be sung with different notes at the same time and will create a unique listening experience. A fun technique to try is to keep your lips closed, place your tongue on the roof of your mouth and begin to hum. Hmm . . . Raise the breath through your nose into your head while humming and you feel the vibration in your nose and back/top of the head.

If you open your mouth, loosen the tongue and sound a low note from your chest. Ah . . . You will feel the vibration in your chest and in your throat. If you sing a very high note, you will feel the vibration in your head. It is fun to play with vibration.

Vibrato is natural in the human singing voice. Most people don't use extensive vibrato, but it is quickly learned. When you sing a straight note, just imagine your voice going a little bit above the note and a little bit below the note. Instead of being straight across the board, the voice vibrates up and down around the note being sung. This is vibrato.

This will help your voice from become too monotone or from becoming too hoarse when singing a lot. Just practice a note going up and down from it just a bit.

Some singers use a lot of vibrato. Too much vibrato can interrupt the flow of the music, especially when singing in duets, but it can also greatly enhance a soloist's performance.

There is also vibration in the voice itself, in the vocal cords. The frequency at which the voice vibrates is another factor. The vocal cords (vocal folds) in your throat are the mucus membrane that is stretched horizontally across the larynx. They vibrate when you speak or when you sing.

A person's vocal pitch can be determined by the frequency and the resonance in these vocal folds. In the adult male, the frequency of this resonance is much lower than in the adult female. And in children it is at a higher frequency. Men usually have a lower-pitched voice with larger vocal cords, and females typically have smaller vocal cords and speak/sing at a higher pitch. So the frequency of the vocal cords vibrating will create different sounds, notes and pitch. Pitch is the frequency of a sound that you hear from the voice.

Although we might say that a person has absolute or perfect pitch, and believe this ability to be natural, the recognition of different notes and the ability to label them and sing them from sheet music usually takes musical training. The ability to sing perfectly on pitch is when a person can hit and hold a note that is played on the piano. We say pitch is *exact* when you are singing the notes that are being played. Often our voices will be a little bit sharp or flat. Here's a visualization that will help you stay on pitch:

Visualize: Close your eyes and take a deep breath, then release the breath. Imagine a very thin tightrope in front of you. You are standing on one platform and must walk the tightrope to the other platform. Imagine that you put your right foot in front of your left foot on the tightrope and you get your balance. When you feel balanced, imagine that you put your left foot in front of your right foot on the tightrope and again you are perfectly balanced. The tightrope is very taut. There is not any "give" in this line of rope. Continue to put one foot in front of the other until you reach the second platform. When you are successfully at the other platform, turn around and see where you have come from.

Now imagine that your voice is like a tightrope. Pick a note, any note and begin to vocalize this note. Stay on this note as if you have walked the tightrope of your voice perfectly. From one platform to the next, hold this note. Project your voice from platform A to platform B in one straight tightrope-like walk across. See your voice make it successfully across the tightrope to the second platform.

Open your eyes and sing a note for twenty seconds. Watch the clock. Take a deep breath and vocalize one note for twenty seconds. See, you can do it. You can sing a note for twenty seconds. Each day sing a note for twenty seconds or more. Enjoy your singing voice, your pitch. If you have an instrument or a mouth tuner, play a note and hold this note with your voice for twenty seconds or more. If necessary, go back to the visualization of walking the tightrope.

The timbre of your vocal quality is sometimes referred to as its tonal color. Sing a note and observe its have richness or roughness, produced by various techniques of the vocal

cords, and the mouth, the tongue, or the lips . . . the timbre is how we as listeners might define the quality of the vocals being sung.

The rhythm of the music is the pattern or the beats within the music. The beats create the rhythm of a song. So when singing a song, you will meet the pitch of the notes, stay up with the rhythm, and take into consideration your own vocal timbre and vibrato, thus creating a unique musical sound all your own.

Whatever you bring with your voice, within the singing, creates your own instrument for making music.

Each one of these categories can change and influence the sound, the feeling, the expression and the experience of the song being sung. If you listen to the voice of Billie Holiday, you will notice that her timbre is very deep and scratchy. Her vibrato is extensive. Someone else singing the same song, say *Summertime* from Porgy and Bess, would sound different. Ms. Holliday's voice would be considered the jazzy rendition of the song, whereas the crooning vocals of Frank Sinatra have a smoother feel.

MUSIC AND COLOR

The connections between color, numbers, and notes on the octave scale could be considered metaphysical in nature. Each note within an octave can be correlated with a color from the color spectrum and a number. Some people I've talked to envision color to represent notes when they sing and numbers for the beat or rhythm in a song.

It is suggested that color could correspond to the notes: C=Red, D=Orange, E=Yellow, F=Green, G=Blue, A=Indigo, B=Violet. There are seven notes in an octave and seven primary colors in the rainbow. And also seven whole notes of an octave relative to seven days of the week, and as well twelve half-notes proportional to twelve months of the year.

In short, there are just too many synchronicities and electromagnetic connections occurring between music and life itself to ignore. It's interesting research, and you can learn more about it in the resources section of this book.

Music is an integral piece of our existence; it's probably far more important to us than we even begin to understand.

So it's important for us to enjoy it as an everyday part of our lives and *not* take it for granted. Singing brings music from inside ourselves to the world around us, and helps us integrate the "cosmos" inside our material bodies (body, mind, spirit). Color can help us stay on pitch.

Here is a visualization to help you feel the connection between color and the notes.

Colored Pitch Visualization: Close your eyes. Take a deep breath; hold it for a second, and then release it. Make sure that your breathing is even and full. Visualize a color; whatever color comes to mind is perfect. Make sure that the color is very vivid in your mind. Now imagine there's a note that goes along with this color. Begin to vocalize that note. Either hum the note or sing it out.

When you are singing this note, imagine your voice going up just a bit from this note, perhaps to the next higher note. Imagine the color changing along with the change of the note. See that new color. Now step it back down to the original note you were vocalizing and go back to the first color. Now go a step lower with the note, and see another color change. Perhaps when you were singing the lower note you saw a darker color. Or perhaps you saw gradations of the same color. Or maybe you see singly different colors with each note. Practice this meditation using different notes and different colors.

A variation on this meditation is that you are seeing the note and seeing the color. You can add brightness to the color by adding a variant of imaginary light to the color. This may change the richness of the note that you hum. For instance, if you are humming a C and you see the color royal blue, you can add a bright white light to the royal blue. It will brighten the blue and most likely brighten the note that you are singing.

Do this meditation often to amplify and moderate the pitch in your voice with the use of color.

MUSIC, LEARNING, AND ATHLETICS

Let's look at baroque music and how it influences mood, learning, and attitude. A 1996 study by the College Entrance Examination Board determined that students who sang or played an instrument growing up scored fifty-one percent higher on the verbal part of the SAT exam and thirty-nine percent higher on math.

Baroque music (music that includes the works of Bach and Mozart and was composed during the baroque era, 1600 to 1759) appears to have positive effects on learning in both children and adults, as evidenced by work done at the University of California at Irvine. Albert Einstein reportedly became smarter because he learned how to play the violin and listened to Mozart and Bach. He often improvised on the violin to help figure out his theorems.

Baroque music has sixty beats per minute. That pattern seems to relax the body and the mind to the point that it's easier to retain information. Hence learning is easier while listening to this type of music.

In the counseling profession there is a category of music therapy that has a benefit for many people, especially for those with bipolar disorder and other medical-mental conditions that need a sense of creative musical outlet. Music is essential to our world. And I propose that singing is beneficial to almost every one in every condition. Even for those of limited vocal abilities, the practice of singing is beneficial.

Music can be used as motivation and give you power to succeed in anything. I'm sure many of us have played a particular song or album and felt motivated. I'm also certain that songs come on the radio and give us a certain sense of strength and direction that takes us forward.

Most exercise programs have music associated with them for motivation and comfort level. If you have music playing, the ability to do a few more crunches or lifts is possible. And for the runner, music may enhance the experience of jogging.

Athletes have often used music to help propel themselves in their sport. The use of visualization in achieving what they want to make happen is also important to many athletes. Most successful athletes, in some way, visualize how they are going to make it to their goal. Music may or may not be an influence there, but I suggest if they would sing in their leisure time, they might succeed even more. Singing and vocal training seem to improve breathing, which makes the effort easier for the athlete as well.

Many athletes visualize the run, the game, the swim they are about to undertake. They visualize their own actions; they prepare themselves through visualization the possible actions of others. Adding music to visualization can also help one relax. Music works as a meditation incentive; when the athlete is visualizing, his or her mind and body are more at rest.

Music during visualization can make the visual become clearer; more possibilities can come into play. The athlete can work out any kinks before entering the competition. If the athlete prepares for this event by visualizing, he or she can pick suitable music for the competition to get maximum results. The mood can be enhanced for the actual event by the music chosen.

For the more sedate person, music may calm the physical, emotional being enough that you may be able to hear the callings of your inner being, the soul. I always advocate meditation. Not all of us are able to meditate, but music can help us relax and hence become meditative. Music can also help us contemplate, and this alone helps the mind clear itself of excess baggage.

It doesn't matter whether you are skilled in music, have a good voice, know a lot about music, or if you are simply interested in singing a song for your own happiness and well-being. I say sing whenever possible.

Music is moonlight in the gloomy night of life.
—JEAN PAUL RICHTER (1763–1825)

POWER SINGING

I've always had a strong voice, but it's not always stable or on-pitch. At least I can belt out a song, but it's not always the most pleasant for others to listen to. Therefore when I speak of power-singing, it has nothing to do with how loud the voice is, but rather with the way singing makes you feel. If someone else is singing and it makes you feel powerful inside, then—for you—that person is power-singing. If you are doing the singing and you begin to feel strong and powerful, then you are power-singing.

One artist that I love to listen to and watch is Andrea Bocelli. He has such a beautiful tremolo in his voice and can powerhouse some awesome high notes. His splendid pitch and operatic presence, always consistent, combined with the (usually) quite loud power in his song, sends shivers up my spine. For me he is a power singer.

Some of today's rap artists, like Eminem, Lil' Whyte, and Missy Elliot, keep younger audiences as well as some of the older crowd in the lyrical flow of the music. When I listen to this music, I immediately want to move around. Hip-hop is a culture about which I very know little, but it does have my interest. Its dramatic voice deserves recognition. This is the type of music that definitely lends itself to DJ mastership and poetic expression. It has a place in the Hall of Music Fame for sure. And I would call this music, because of its vocal presence, power-singing.

THE DRUMMER'S BEAT

What would music be without the rhythmic beat of the drums? In fact, drumming alone can produce a notable composition. Some of my favorite drummers throughout my generation were Sandy Nelson and Buddy Rich. Not to mention many of the greats rock and rollers, legend Ringo Starr of the Beatles, world-renown Rolling Stones drummer Charlie Watts, and Led Zeppelin's infamous John Bonham 1948–1980. A good drum solo or competition is hard to beat (no pun intended).

My husband John used to set up drums for a band. Back in his day, drums actually had skins made out of all types of materials from different types of animal hides to synthetic membrane-like substances. Today most drum skins are made out of a synthetic plastic matter. Tuning the drums would begin with each drum being set with a higher note on the outside and be tuned to sound the same note but at a lower octave at the inside of the drum. The smaller drums of course resonate at a higher pitch than the larger drums. In drum wars, one person might have all drums set for E and the other might be set at G, giving them each a distinct sound throughout the competition.

The beat of a band is kept by the drummer, but a song can be found even within the drum solo. The consistency of a song or rhythm is usually kept by the instrumentation, but the voice is also an instrument. Singing can be the constant.

Most music uses drums for beat, instrumentation for rhythm, and vocals for flair. However, in some songs, we hear only the vocals and the drummer's beat (no instrumentation) with the song being sung to the beat. The a Capella performance has the voice keeping all three, the rhythm, the flair and the instrumentation alive.

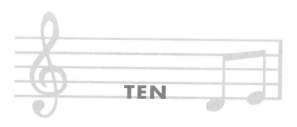

TEN

Sweet Songs

Words make you think a thought. Music makes you feel a feeling. A song makes you feel a thought.

—EDGAR YIPSEL HARBURG

Love cannot express the idea of music, while music may give an idea of love.

—LOUIS-HECTOR BERLIOZ

ROMANTIC MELODIES

My Uncle Satchmo

One of my earliest memories is of spending time with my Uncle Jack. He used to take me down to the club on Sunday afternoon; "the club" was the Red Dog Saloon where he bartended during the week—and jammed with his friends on Sundays, when the bar was closed to the public. He could imitate Louis "Satchmo" Armstrong perfectly, even down to the magnificent trumpet solos.

That trumpet would blare, and my uncle's mouth almost grew as big as Satchmo's (who was nicknamed for his satchel-mouth). This is where I learned about music. Here, in my small-town life, I had a big-town sound going on around me every Sunday, starting when I was only four years old.

I still play Louis Armstrong when I want to feel romantic. *Oh, When the Saints* or *What a Wonderful World* . . . they still can bring up passion inside me, just as they did so many years ago.

I'm grateful to have been exposed to such great talent so early on. Uncle "Satchmo" Jack even wrote a song for me when I was born. He was overseas in the military at the time:

The house on Rose Street contains one so sweet, the girl I'd surely like to see. Her name is Julie. I love her truly, the girl with whom I'd love to be. She'd take your heart by storm with her sweet smile so warm. There's no one in the world like she. Tho' I have never met her, I can't forget her. Yes she, yes she's the girl for me.
—JOHN HAROLD KENNEDY, 1957.

Sealed with a Kiss

Music melts all the separate parts of our bodies together.
—ANAIS NIN

It was the summer of 1972, and I was fourteen years old. My father had taken a job in North Dakota for the summer, and if we wanted to see him, we had to travel there to do it. He was working with another man from the area, so the two wives, six girls, and one boy had to take a long, arduous drive to the campground where the men were staying. The campground was out in the middle of nowhere, some twenty-five miles from the nearest town. This meant that we had to find our own entertainment.

During our stay there, I met a boy named Michael. He was very sweet to me. He said he had fallen in love with me the moment he saw me. He was seventeen . . . wow! Every time we were together, it seemed, the Bobby Vinton cover of *Sealed with a Kiss* was playing on the radio. This was a remote part of North Dakota, so to have a radio at all was impressive, but Michael seemed to always have a radio with him.

The two girls I was with also met boys, friends of Michael's. We shared most of our time together as a group, though sometimes Michael and I spent moments alone in the woods. We became very close, very connected, and talked about everything. He was very good to me, and I loved him dearly. The other two girls also had crushes on the boys they had met, so you might say that when we parted toward the end of the summer, we were living the song.

In accordance with the song, Michael promised to write to me every day and seal the letter with a kiss, and he did for many weeks after that. He went home to Washington. I went back to Minnesota with my family. But I cried for many years after that whenever I heard the song *Sealed with a Kiss*. Because of the song, we made a pact to meet that next September, but that never happened.

To this day, whenever I hear *Sealed with a Kiss,* I just smile and feel good. Michael was my first love and my first heartache. It prepared me for many more wonderful and broken relationships in my life, but I always seal them with a kiss before they end. This is certainly a song strongly attached to a memory.

Lost Love

A poem by Jules

You do not know my heartache. You do not know
my pain.
You also do not know my joy, my passion or disdain.
You only begin to know me, as you start to see
The song within me, filling my heart with glee.

The curtain is open very rarely for a peek
Look inside of me, so that I can speak
The pains, the sorrows, the gladness and the bliss
No brighter tomorrow, as this moment we kiss.

So I send you wandering, far and farther away
Because you do not want me and why for this I pray?
Little is understood from where you stand, lonelier
by each day
I ask you then, why do you run from me, please
I beg you, stay.

You glance, you smile, you open your heart
A tear I see welling up, if only you could start
To see the pain and joy in me as I have you near
But you will not listen, because you have this fear.

An angst that takes you far away, to a land I cannot roam
Blessed be the angels there, because they accept you
    home
My hearth, my spirit dwells only upon this Earth
By the age comes death, but first I must rebirth.

My truth, my heart shall bear
Only with you trodden there
Take my soul and leave me dry
For only you love, shall I cry.

Visualize: here is a visualization exercise that may help create flow in your life. Pick out some very comfortable quiet music and put it on your stereo or headset. Adjust your body in a lying or sitting position so that you feel at ease, and begin to notice your breathing. Take a deep breath in, and then release it. Take a few more deep breaths until you feel serene. Put all stressful thoughts out of your mind. All disturbances are far, far away. Inhale through your nose, and exhale through your mouth, releasing all negativity in your body on the out-breath.

Now imagine that you are standing inside the music. On all sides of you, music is flowing like a golden liquid. It is warm and thick and flows like a waterfall that starts above the top of your head and runs down your head, your shoulders. It trickles down to your arms, your throat, your chest, stomach, down your legs, all the way to your toes. This golden liquid music is healing your body and spirit. Feel it washing away the cares and anxieties that are in your body.

You may sit in this meditation space as long as you like,

and when you return to a more awakened state of consciousness, notice the calmness that you feel. Take this calm into your day.

THE SACRED OHM

The Ohm or Aum is a sacred part of many religious philosophies. Some believe it to be creation's most basic and primal sound.

The correct pronunciation of the Aum would have us starting by resonating the A sound, which comes out of the throat (ahhh). When we move to the U (ooooo) sound, it comes from the stomach region, down low. Then you pronounce the M (mmmm) with the sound coming out from the lips. So, complete, it starts at the throat, down toward the navel and ends by coming out of the lips: Aaa . . . oooo . . . mmm. Hold the note.

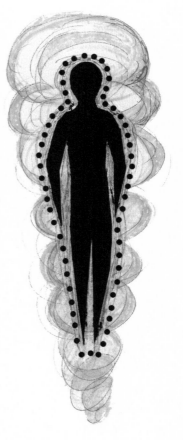

In many different traditions the Ohm is used for mantras. Whenever I have been involved in a group sounding of the Aum, I feel a very powerful connection to my inner being and the other beings in the room. We begin to sound like one voice, and of course that is my aim in recruiting people to sing and express themselves.

Eventually we will all be singing the same song with the same voice. It's said that a group of people vocalizing the Ohm together in sync will also find that their heartbeats are synchronized. When singing the Ohm, it is easy for the body to produce enough oxygen to carry the sound for long periods of time. In the group pronouncing the Ohm, there is a constant. One person from the group can stop to take a breath, but the rest of the group carries it through so there's no break in the sound.

CHANTING AND PRAYER SINGING

Chanting is the continuous recitation of different words or sounds. Many believe that chanting can create an altered state of consciousness. Many faiths and philosophies have chants used for meditation, prayer, preparation for rites of passage, and for healing or hunting activities. I can attest to the results I've achieved personally when I've used the Ohm, either when chanting or listening to chant in ceremony. It helps me feel centered, powerful—and filled with pleasure.

Overtone singing is another type of chanting or harmonic singing. The most recognizable form of this type of vocalizing is the throat singing of Mongolia, called Khoomii. The sound of throat singing seems to be low hums matched with very high-pitched sounds. This is done by manipulating and amplifying the hum and changing the shape of the mouth, the larynx, and the pharynx (thus doubling the vocal folds).

This allows the singer to sound more than one pitch at a time. A study of chanting Tibetan monks found that the state of their brainwaves while engaging in chant were much the same as a person in very deep meditation. Of course, the monks use the chanting as a form of meditation.

The rosary, when recited by Catholics before mass, can sound much like a chant. Normally a cantor is at the front of the church and recites the first lines of the prayer associated with the rosary bead, and then the congregation finishes the prayer. It becomes very chant-like, meditative, and even hypnotic.

I encourage you to try chanting either the Ohm or some other word or sound. If you use chanting already as a part of your practice, I'd suggest trying something different from what you might be doing already, to challenge yourself. Find something that suits you and begin to chant your personal mantra.

HARMONY AND PART SINGING

I love the song *Mister Sandman*. I originally heard it sung on television by the Andrew Sisters. I loved the way their voices harmonized. My grandmother sang along with the sisters—not exactly on key, but she sang along and danced a little jig in the living room. The song holds good memories, and I was excited to hear it recorded again in 1999 on the Trio II album by Emmylou Harris, Dolly Parton, and Linda Ronstadt.

One verse of *Daddy Sang Bass,* written by Carl Perkins in 1968 and most notably performed by Johnny Cash, the

Carter Family and the Statler Brothers, actually tells how harmony works. It celebrates the help that singing—especially singing in a family context—brings to a troubled soul. Indeed, some of the world's most beautiful music has come out of trouble, sadness, and the stress of poverty. It's a way to bring the family together, have some fun, and relieve everyday weariness.

Singing a harmony part, either above or below the vocalist singing the primary tune, can be easy if you have an ear for harmony. But it's a skill that can also be learned.

My sister Sarah thinks that Diamond Rio has some of the best harmonies she has ever heard. My husband John likes the Righteous Brothers' harmonies, especially in *Unchained Melody*. I'm a fan of some of the folk-music types of harmonies of the Indigo Girls, the Weavers, and some Appalachian mountain music. I love listening to harmonies, yet have a difficult time singing harmony myself, because I lose track of my own voice when singing something different from my neighbor. It takes practice and time to sing harmony, but it sure creates a wonderful sound when it is perfected!

SINGING WITH CONFIDENCE

What can I say about confidence? There's no one who can give it to you. I've sometimes been about to sing or give a lecture and found myself wanting in the worst way to back down from it. I understand not having the confidence to speak in public: add singing to the mix, though, and it can produce even more anxiety!

Many people have negative programming from childhood about their singing voices. Many of these people shut down and never sing in public. We may have been told to be quiet when we chose to sing, or we may have been laughed at, or we may have never had the chance to sing with others nearby.

But let's change all that! Let's be brave and sing! No one can help you have confidence enough to do anything. This is a power that has to come from within, but there are things we can all do to alleviate performance anxiety. Breathing properly will help.

There are many ways a person can learn to sing well. One of my favorites is to take a note and begin to vocalize it to the vowels: aaaa . . . eeee . . . iiiii . . . oooo . . . uuuu. Then do the same with other notes. Remember to take a good breath before you begin each note.

Breathing is important for singing. Begin this exercise by standing or sitting up straight on the edge of the chair, shoulders back. Stand up if you can to get a true feel for this technique. Take a breath deep into your chest. Feel your chest fill up and rise with air. Release the breath. Now take another deep breath, pulling it down toward your stomach. Put your hands on your waist when you inhale. A good breath in for this exercise and you'll feel even your sides expand. This may take some practice.

Now breathe in to the count of five (remember to pull it all the way down to your stomach, expanding even your sides), stop the breath for two counts, and then release the breath for five counts. Do this breath five times. Then change the out-breath count to ten, so that you're releasing the breath and pushing all the air out of your stomach. This exercise will help you hold notes longer and take fewer breaths while singing longer phrases.

You can also visualize doing a great performance before you sing in public. Add a little light to the visualization so that the music is light-filled. Imagine the audience cheering and wanting more. Then breathe and feel good about yourself. You can do it. Just get out there and sing!

Here's a little ditty about *Doubty Duties*. Whenever doubts start to fill your head and heart, remember that they are there because they think they have a duty to fulfill. They've been with you so long that they do not know when they are no longer needed:

DOUBTY DUTIES

The *doubties* are little creatures that come into your reality when you least expect them. They are the little doubts that hide in your subconscious waiting to attack at your most vulnerable moments. They come in, multiply, and eat everything in sight that has a positive edge to it. Don't let the doubties eat you alive! Take control now with meditation, clarity, and humor. Wipe the darn things off the map. Don't let them into your positive arena at all. When a doubty comes into your awareness, talk to it nicely. Tell it, "I don't need you anymore," or "would you kindly go elsewhere to do your deed, please?"

There are plenty of duties a doubty could do, like take a nap for you, or spit on your shoes and then polish them. Doubties make good house pets if you leave them alone to do what they are good at: doubting. When they've doubted enough, they'll come home to rest on your laurels. Just let them flounder around being what they are—and you continue to believe in yourself and your highest potential anyway! A doubty's duties are to keep you positive by using the well-known force of reverse psychology. "I don't think I can," (doubty in full form) "perhaps I can," (doubty strength weakening) "I know I can," (doubty conquered!).

When you're singing, if the doubties come up, wash them away with a little "I know I can!"

ADVICE FROM THE PROS

Lisa Germano (interviewed in chapter one) says to "exercise the tongue." That's her most important counsel for singing. She claims that if your tongue is loose, everything else will fall into place. To exercise the tongue, just move it in and out of your mouth and around while making singing noises.

I like to go up and down the scale a few times to clear my throat and just get the voice in working condition. Sometimes I slide way up and don't come down in any order to challenge my voice to a workout.

Sarah Ennis Zak (interviewed in chapter seven) says, "Before singing, don't drink milk or carbonated soda. They coat your throat and make it harder to vocalize. Drink lemon water. That always clears the throat. Also, limber up the body with a few exercises," she adds. Here are some ways you can do that: Move your head around to loosen the shoulders. Stretch the body all over to feel good, and then get out there and sing!

PROTECTING THE VOICE

I guess I'd say that my voice is my greatest asset. Since I do counseling mostly by phone, and I want to continue to sing, I need my voice. It is my instrument, and I must fine-tune and preserve it.

To keep your voice in good shape:

- Limit the time you spend talking needlessly to others. It's good to have social interactions, but to preserve the integrity of my voice and my reputation, I don't engage in idle gossip and I don't complain. I believe too much in the concept of karma, that what goes around comes around. So if I make unfair judgments about people and then spread that around, it's likely my subsequent karma will jeopardize my voice's quality.

- Choose not to yell, scream or squeal. Your voice cannot take this kind of strain.

- Stay away from hazardous chemicals and odors as much as possible.

- Do your best to get as much rest as possible, especially if you need to use your voice in performance or for work. Fatigue takes its toll on all aspects of bodily functions.

- Eat well and exercise. (I fall slack on these quite often, but I know better. When I eat right and get some moderate and pleasant exercise, my whole body and attitude are in good condition.)

- Do breathing exercises, as instructed throughout this book. Breathing helps support the voice.

- Visualizing helps keep you balanced and positive. When life is going well, your voice will sound upbeat and alive.

- Some women cannot sing well when they are a few days pre-menstrual. I've always taken this into consideration and found it to be very true. Take good care during these days not to strain your voice. In the same vein, when you have a cold or illness, protect your voice by using it as little as possible.

- Do vocal practice before a performance, and rest your voice after a performance.

ELEVEN

Song in Religion

> Music is my religion.
> —JIMI HENDRIX

Almost all religious services use song to enhance the worship experience. Each religion, denomination, and/or spiritual philosophy followed in community uses some song structure to add to the service, meditation or gathering. As an interested student of spiritual thought, I have joined in the practice of various types of religions.

In this next section, I'll share my personal experiences with music and song used in these religions as well as some technical knowledge I have garnered through research. Song seems to be an integral part of the way that religions bring people to a higher level of emotional connectedness and joy.

GROWING UP AMERICAN CATHOLIC— *AVE MARIA* TO POLKA

As a young person growing up in the Midwest, church

services were a big part of our weekly routine. My parents raised me Catholic, although three of *their* parents were of other religions. We never missed a Sunday mass unless we were so sick we couldn't get out of bed. Mass was always said in Latin then—Vatican II with its liturgical changes (including mass in the vernacular) was not until 1965. Until then, all liturgical songs were also sung in Latin. My favorite Latin hymn to this day is the *Ave Maria*. Translated into English, the *Ave Maria* becomes the primary prayer to the Blessed Mother, the *Hail Mary*.

Sarah Brightman performs an absolutely fabulous rendition of the *Ave Maria* on her album *The Classics: Best of Sarah Brightman*. The music is so fluid and seems the epitome of grace and beauty, not only of Catholic traditional mysticism but of life—as it, too, is mysterious.

In my youth I was afraid of the large stone building that we called church. Inside the structure was a mysterious world of dialect and passionate ritual I could never understand. The music was the only piece of that world I could relate to. It was elegant and uplifting. Latin was easy to sing, just not so easy to understand!

After Vatican II many songs were translated into and sung in English. These lyrics seemed boorish and harsh to me. I no longer enjoyed singing at Mass . . . at least, not until the Polka Mass was introduced in our church. What better way to get those Minnesota Catholics into church but with a polka band!

Remnants of the "Beer Barrel" polka now became the "Jesus Loves Me" polka. It was always fun in those days to go to church and listen to the live polka band, especially on

Saturday afternoon at the five o'clock mass. I always wondered whether the band played for mass at five o'clock and at a wedding party at eight that same evening!

Things changed even more after that when they began to have rock masses. A group of young musicians calling themselves a rock band would extract their Catholic band members and send them over to the church for the five o'clock Saturday mass. A few religious rock ballads later, they too were free to join again with the larger band for the Saturday night gig at the high school or birthday party.

Those were the days of experimentation. Today, masses like these are still offered around the country. They enlighten parishioners with alternatives to their ordinary religious experience.

MY MULTI-DENOMINATIONAL FAMILY— LUTHERAN TO BAPTIST

As noted earlier, not all of my grandparents were Catholic. My maternal grandmother was Lutheran and my paternal grandparents were Episcopalian. It was only my deceased maternal grandfather who was Catholic, and so my mother was raised in that faith. I often went to the Lutheran church with my grandmother, and then would also attend Catholic mass the same day. I also attended the Episcopal services for various events.

My in-laws in my early married days were Baptists, so I attended services in that denomination as well. Except for the change in the ritualistic parts of the service, I found all of them to be much the same and the music to be similar—

except for one big difference in the actual singing of the music. In the church in which I grew up, we always sang just two verses of each song. In most of the Protestant churches I have attended over the years, the songbooks are not closed until each and every verse of the song is sung. I found myself many times shutting the hymnal and waiting for the sermon while the congregation just kept on singing!

MEDITATIVE CHANT—ZEN RETREAT TO THE DALAI LAMA

When I was in my mid-twenties I began to research and experiment with other traditions beyond the Christian churches to which I'd previously been exposed. In fact, I had to travel many miles from my hometown to find these religious opportunities.

My first experience with "outside" religions was with Buddhism. I found the principles and philosophy much to my spiritual liking, plus I found forms of deep meditation that were refreshing and enlightening. I went on my first Zen Buddhist retreat when I was twenty-six years old. It was a three-day walking and sitting meditation: except for brief moments of spiritual instruction (including some chanting and chimes) throughout the weekend, participants were required to function in total silence. Three days of meditation, watching thoughts but not attaching to them. In all activity we were to be contemplative and have no verbal or interactive communication with each another.

I found that although the meditation was very good for me, and I still practice different forms of meditation, I missed the music. I heard music playing in my thoughts all the time and had to work to let it go according to the practice. I guess I could say I have a musical mind, as it wouldn't give it up even for Zen!

The chanting done in most forms of Buddhism is a mantra or prayer that brings the devotee to a higher level of reverence and prepares the mind for meditation. I had the tremendous honor a few years ago to sit with the Dalai Lama during a prayer session and one of his divine talks addressed to monks and local students living on the campus. Those of us in attendance who were not close to that level, and those (like me) who were not Buddhist, sat outside under a tent. There were television cameras placed around the tent so that everyone could watch, listen to, and participate in the event.

The Dalai Lama and the monks began their chanting session. I watched his face closely on the screen. I have rarely seen this man without a smile of some sort across his face. He makes me smile, and I feel a breath of compassion radiating from his soul. No matter what happens to him, his people, and humanity at large, there is always joy exuding from his heart.

During the chanting session I noticed him looking across the room; he began to laugh. Within his chant there is a giggle that doesn't stop. His compassion had me in tears until this moment, but once he started laughing, I had to laugh with him. What jovialness and sense of spirit he has! What truth he shows to his followers!

The chanting continued more solemnly from that point forward, and I too was carried into contemplative consciousness. This is a form of song that has a great deal of power associated with it. I don't know what the mantra is, what it stands for, or how to chant it, but I do know it functions as a catalyst for many to obtain a higher state of relaxation and spirituality.

HYMNS TO GOSPEL—AMY GRANT TO ELVIS

A hymn is a song written as a devotion to a god or some other type of (religious or secular) idol. The hymnist is the writer of hymns. Hymnody is the singing of hymns, or a group of hymns that are sung by a community within a religion or sect. Hymns are composed within all philo-sophical/spiritual beliefs, from the ancient Greek Homer's *Odyssey* to the more current devotional rock music of artists like Amy Grant.

I was first exposed to Ms. Grant's music during a vocal lesson in 1977, when my new voice teacher thought it would be good for me to learn some pieces from her repertoire. I had no idea who Amy Grant was, and the vocal teacher was appalled. She quickly brought out sheet music and began to play the piano accompaniment. The range in Ms. Grant's voice is phenomenal, and I found that I couldn't reach the soprano notes at the high end. After three grueling weeks of trying to make my voice accommodate my vocal teacher's requests, I gave it up.

Lisa Germano was right. "Don't believe any particular rules about singing," especially when you just want to sing for fun and the love of life. Although I was unable to sing like Amy Grant, her Christian hymns and popular music over the years have delighted millions of listeners time and again. She has an amazing voice and an awesome talent for songwriting.

The year 1977 was the end of an era, as it was the year Elvis Presley—singer of rock and roll, but also of gospel music—died. His mother, Gladys Presley, was a lover of gospel music, and Elvis had the perfect voice and temperament for singing songs like *How Great Thou Art* (1967 Grammy Winner Best Sacred Performance album) and *Amazing Grace.* He won many Grammy awards for gospel music.

Gospel music was modeled on traditional African-American spirituals sung in the late 1800s. Thomas Dorsey (composer of *Peace in the Valley*) is considered the "father of gospel music." He blended traditional religious music with blues and jazz. He was shunned for much of his life, as many preachers and churchgoers considered his music the work of the devil. Gospel is a freeform type of musical expression, often spontaneous, but always sung with spiritual inspiration and devotion.

In the 1970s, gospel music started to gain mainstream popularity. Today gospel music goes beyond religious or spiritual music and has hit the mainstream with artists like Yolanda Adams singing *Day By Day* and other popular gospel tunes. In my mind, all music is spiritual if it brings me to a higher level of action and feeling.

A hymn is the praise of God with song;
a song is the exultation of the mind dwelling on
eternal things, bursting forth in the voice.

—THOMAS AQUINAS

As I began to delve into this study of music in religious traditions, I was amazed at how much of the music is similar in nature, that hymns are used almost universally, and that most religions employ some sort of chanting or ritualistic verse within their ceremonies. Each song that I sang within every tradition had meaning for me on a very deep level, much like the national anthems did for me when I did the research for that chapter.

I suggest that if you are searching for meaning in your life, find a church, synagogue, or spiritual ceremony of some type that involves singing and begin to explore the deeper side of your soul through ritual and music.

TWELVE

Singing Fun

Anything that is too stupid to be spoken is sung.

—Voltaire

PARTY TIME—THE MINNESOTA EXPERIENCE

Okay, to be honest now . . . I grew up in Minnesota, right?—the "Land of Ten Thousand Lakes" that freeze over as thick as you-know-what in the heart of January! "Can't drive the car out on the lake until the ice is at least—oh—six feet thick!" is the motto. Well, then, in my opinion, that's the time to stay home, or take a brisk walk to the neighborhood tavern—not be out on the lake, for gosh sake!

When I was a young adult of legal drinking age, it was rather fun to go to the local piano bar down the street for some tunes and social time. My best time was when the "piano guy" Dave would ask me to take the microphone and sing my favorite song, *The Rose*. Since I'm short, I had to stand on a chair beside the grand piano and put my lips to the microphone. I sang this song that touches my heart so much, with the crowd cheering and giving me a standing ovation when I finished . . . every time. Do I remember the performances? Uh, not really. I'm told they were good. Rarely have I had nights like those since. And I don't drink in public any more, at least not in a piano or karaoke bar. It's too dangerous!

How, you ask? Well, let's consider the night my sister and I sang tribute to our wonderful mother—in a biker bar on karaoke night after last call on drinks. That must have been oh, so pleasant for the two remaining bikers, the waitress and bartender. It's amazing they didn't have the bouncer pull us offstage and put us in a taxi! I still blush at the thought and would never advocate this type of excess to anyone, but the image of two thirty-something-year-old sisters discussing their mother in such an endearing manner and then singing songs like *Que Sera, Sera* in our drunken state must have had them rolling in the aisles!

At this point in my life I'd do well to have a glass of wine and still be able to sing. Alcohol in large quantities is not good for one's singing voice, and it encourages my ego to a place that promises *your voice is wonderful just as it is, sing louder, not better.* Really not flattering at all.

How embarrassing is that? It's no way to build confidence, that's for sure: a drink to relax—well ... maybe. But for me, never before a performance of any type. It just isn't worth the excess phlegm and mucus in my throat, and the embarrassing moments of uncontrolled behavior.

Television, a good book, and some relaxing music (or *Prairie Home Companion* on the radio) in the background is much more to my liking these days. I don't need a microphone and a bunch of drinkers to give credence to my voice and song. But karaoke can be fun, and I'm sure many people have some excellent stories to tell about karaoke night at their favorite pub. They could fill a book all by themselves, I'm certain!

Nothing is more fun than a good, ol' down-home hootenanny. What am I talking about? Well, in my interpretation, a hootenanny is simply a party with some good live folk, jazz, or country music playing all the while, and a lot of jamming going on—family musicians and friends blending their instruments, and perhaps a singer or two mixed in.

These parties were usually held in someone's barn or machine shed, often in the late spring or early fall. Sometimes neighborhoods would throw a block party: shut down the street, throw up some tents, and put up a stage. All sorts of talent showed up at these lively events. We all prayed for clear skies and moderately warm temperatures and would dance and sing until dawn. A hootenanny is a gathering of community playing music and enjoying one another. Many stories are shared, the food is awesome, and the music—fine!

DELIGHTFUL CHILDREN'S TUNES

> Fantasy, if it's really convincing, can't become dated
> for the simple reason that it represents a flight into
> a dimension that lies beyond the reach of time.
> —WALT DISNEY

By the time my son was four years old, he was very familiar with Big Bird, Oscar the Grouch, and all the other *Sesame*

Street characters. He'd begin to stare at the clock roughly four minutes before the start of his favorite show, wait until the big hand hit the twelve, and run to the television to turn on *Sesame Street*.

He did this four times a day until he went off to school. He and his sister rarely missed a program, and I could not forget the music for many years after they grew out of the Muppet phase of life. I still remember *Me and My Lama* every time I see one of the wooly creatures, and *There's a hole in the bucket, dear Liza, dear Liza* . . . you'd have to have been there to understand that children's shows drive a sentimental dichotomy in the heart of any parent who had to listen to them day after day.

When these repetitive days and programs were happening I wondered when, if ever, they would end. Then suddenly they did—and now I miss them. I miss Big Bird singing *Everyone Makes Mistakes* and *The Noodle Song*.

Now, as a grandmother, I am researching and watching songs from the *Blues Clues* program, because I myself haven't got a clue. I've found that the characters and songs that little ones enjoy today are truly much the same as they always were, just with different disguises and musical inflections.

The tunes they play while they exhibit numbers, colors, and letters are in close reflection to the process of visualization we use within this book as singing meditation, only for children with eyes and ears open. The songs are fun to sing and dance to, and the learning happens automatically during this process. Music is such an integral part of our lives from the day we are born.

Before my grandson was born, his daddy would sing to

him in the womb. Less than two minutes after he was born he looked for his father's voice when he heard Daddy singing from the back of the delivery room. To this day he swings his little behind and hums a little tune whenever he hears music, and it always puts a smile on his face.

Music is very important for the development of children. A recent study has shown that children exposed to music at an early age have more perfect pitch and improved cognitive abilities in later years. Children love games set to music: musical instruments, sing-a-longs, musical chairs, and toys that sing or play tunes are all second nature to them. Autistic children are often much more reactive to types of music therapy than to traditional talk therapy because they are more sensitive to the intonations in music and can cognitively interpret vocalizations more readily to music than to standard speech.

Even without the studies, we all must realize that music, and especially singing, is good for the soul. Certainly Walt Disney knew the necessity of music and used it to enliven the Disney adventure lands and cartoon character displays of barnyard humor. Mickey Mouse was introduced by Disney back in 1928. Mickey could play the violin, as he does in his cartoon short *Just Mickey* where he plays the *William Tell Overture*.

Mickey and his friends lead us on wild adventures through cartoons and eventually into the fantasylands of Disneyland (California), Disneyworld (Florida), and Disneyland (Paris and Tokyo). One is never left without a snatch of magical music floating on the air, popular Disney songs like *When You Wish Upon A Star* and *Bibbidi-Bobbidi-Boo*. No one can get away from Disney's world without feeling like a kid at heart. These lands are made magical by the music and the songs. It's hard not to sing along with the small people in *It's a Small World* . . . after all! Imagine the creativity it took to bring this all together. It's a reality all its own and one I wish (upon my star) that everyone, especially children, can enjoy it at least once in their lifetimes.

I recently went to a movie called *Happy Feet* produced by Warner Brothers. Oh, my, what a delightful movie. I'm glad I saw it in a movie theater rather than waiting for the DVD edition. The children in the theater, laughing and screaming at those musical penguins, were a thrill for me all by themselves. The main character, Mumble, could not sing like all the other penguins but—wow! Could he dance. Those happy feet were all over the place. Watch for Ramón, however, because he has a singing voice that is out of this world.

There were a lot of amazing vocalists in this movie as there are in so many of the children-to-adult movies today. The musical scores in these movies must cost more and take more time to write than the storyline. There is so much talent out there and a lot of fun to be had for children today. If used correctly, movies, CDs and computers can be wonderful learning tools for children and give parents and teachers a much-needed break.

CHRISTMAS CAROLS FOR PEACE AND PLEASURE

It is Christmastime as I write this. I remember the times that I went Christmas caroling with the neighbors. It was a delight. We would get all dressed up warm with fancy hats, grab the songbooks, and stroll the local neighborhoods, singing our hearts out to the heavens. After the event we enjoyed delicious hot chocolate, lots of laughter and stories galore. Norman Rockwell, here we come!

One of my favorite movies is *Funny Farm,* starring the comedic actor Chevy Chase. In the movie there is a scene where Chevy offers everyone in the small town money if they'll act like they belong in a Norman Rockwell painting so that he has a better chance of selling his house. The carolers are a delight! They sing day and night with picturesque perfection. I always dreamed life could be like that; a small town of happy folk, all getting along, and carolers singing in the background all year long.

Just the other day I spoke to a woman who works in the local dollar store. She told me that she always used to love the Christmas holiday. She would decorate her house and play Christmas carols all day long for her children. But, she added, since she's been working in retail, her love of the holiday has dissipated. *That is so sad,* I thought. I can see her dilemma. Working with the consumer public must be grueling this time of year. And I'm sure the Christmas carols playing overhead take on a different meaning for her now. Although I, too, have worked in retail, it was never during the Christmas season. I think we should offer our retail workers a round of applause, as they service us very well at this time and always. It's not an easy profession, and they deserve recognition.

Congratulations to you, retail workers of the world. We ought to have a day designated in your honor. And on that day we will play Christmas carols in the background.

My favorite Christmas song is *O Holy Night*, written in 1847 by Adolphe Adam. The music and English lyrics (it was originally in French) combined are so beautiful.

Oh Night Divine is right. Christmas is a time that could be celebrated by all faiths as a time to share love and gratefulness. We could chose a day each year that the world could agree to be at peace. No warfare, no crime. Ah, I'm dreaming perhaps, but it would be wonderful to have a designated day in which everyone promises to do their best to "be quiet" and listen to the heart of the music.

If you listen real closely in the silence there is a carol being sung by the angels. This is my belief, and Christmas carols confirm it for me. I feel reverence when I sing *O Holy Night*, *Silent Night*, and *Joy to the World*. I'm not advocating solely Christianity, but all faiths, and a heartfelt, worldwide state of peace. One day of peace would lead to two, then three . . . and so on.

The world needs a savior indeed, but that savior begins inside each one of us, and song can direct us there. Listen to the music, feel the meaning, sing the songs, and be happy. *Jingle Bells* . . . I'm listening!

CONCLUSION

Living the Song

It occurred to me by intuition, and music was
the driving force behind that intuition. My discovery
was the result of musical perception.

—ALBERT EINSTEIN

Writing this book was an intense emotional experience for me. I love writing and I think I love singing even more, but I've neglected both of these activities for years in my life, to the point I was "almost too old" to think about them. I'm joking about the "too old" part, because we never are too old, but the "almost" part was correct. I've almost been going to write a book all of my life. I've almost been going to sing on stage all of my life. Who cares if I write a book? *Just write.* Who cares if I sing on stage? *Just sing.* I tell you: whatever you want to do in life, *do it*! In one form or another, do it. And someday it *will* become your reality, whether as a career or a hobby . . . or perhaps your entire being.

That is the message I want to convey today. Just sing. Who

cares if what you sing, or how you sing, isn't perfect? Just sing! When people tell me about their aches and pains, I tell them to sing more, to listen to music more, and to visualize light more. In my estimation, each note corresponds to a color of light and light is what will heal this world. Light cannot be present without color, and color cannot be present without the notes that make up the music. I'm not a scientist. Can't prove it myself, but in my heart, this is the truth of it.

I love music, and I'll bet you do, too. I love to sing, and I'll bet you do, too. If we don't allow ourselves to listen to and do what we love, then how are we going to heal our broken hearts and cure our pain, leading to healthy minds, body and spirit? I say, let's create a movement among the people. Let's sing, and sing, and sing, until everything is all right in the world. Don't let that little piece of magic (song) get away from you . . . Sing! Let's live the song!

Without music, life would be a mistake.

FRIEDRICH NIETZSCHE

APPENDIX A

The Music Journal

It's important to be aware of how much music is around us in our lives, including all the sounds that combine to make some form of music. For nine days, pay attention to every time you hear music.

Please visit www.dreamtimepublishing.com/books.php for a downloadable version of this appendix.

On the first three days, don't sing along. Just record the music and your thoughts here:

Day 1:

Day 2:

Day 3:

On the second three days, notice how many times you sing along with the music or want to, and record these situations and thoughts here:

Day 4:

Day 5:

Day 6:

On the last three days, make up and sing your own songs and record your progress here:

Day 7:

Day 8:

Day 9:

Singing Notes:

APPENDIX B

Singing Practice

Please visit www.dreamtimepublishing.com/books.php for a downloadable version of this appendix.

1. Write a sentence here. Any sentence will do.

2. Now sing this sentence in any way you want. Sing the words. And sing it differently (change the notes, intonations, length of notes, etc.) each time.

3. Write what it is like to sing—just any sentence, and be creative with it.

4. Now sing a song that you know, any song to which you know the words and that you like.

5. Without judging your voice, write what it is you like about singing that song.

6. Sing another quick tune, something simple.

7. Write about the experience of singing this song.

8. How does singing help you to express yourself?

9. List some ways you can use singing to improve your life.

APPENDIX C

Singing Experience

Please visit www.dreamtimepublishing.com/books.php for a downloadable version of this appendix.

List your ten favorite songs to sing here. Keep track of why you like these songs.

1.

2.

3.

4.

5.

6.

7.

8.

9.

10.

Add any new songs that you like and want to remember for future reference.

New Song List:

- Record yourself singing. When you listen to the recording, what do you think?

- Sing for someone else (that's right, brave it!). Notice the reactions of people when you start singing out of the blue. Just sing! And get them singing.

- Sing along with someone else. Christmas or holiday songs are familiar to many.

- Sing in unlikely places.

- Sing to children when you come in contact with them.

- Start a singing group.

- Write a song and sing it.

- Do a singing telegram.

- Just sing and open your heart. How does it feel?

- Take a poetry class. Write a poem and begin to sing it!

A Love Forever One

A poem by Jules

The day I met you fear took over
I couldn't look at you,
As love would be I wouldn't see
We as one, but only two

Now this love transcends all time and space
Einstein would be so proud
A love that yearns for truth and place
It speaks so soft and loud.

A love that shares no boundaries
And tells a story too
When we talk about tomorrow
We also wonder who . . .

Will be our love mate then
How will our love evolve
What will make us understand
How the problem's solved

How an aching heart
Can feel so much at rest
Yet beauty in the one I love
Makes this life the best

Hope and so much more
A life worth living for

Peace and fare thee well
Our love is at the door

Waiting to be blossomed
And surely to be caressed
We must begin to see
Our hearts have been oppressed

From tiding to forgiveness
We walk the mighty two
A ninety-year forever
That leaves a mark for you

Take this love my darling
And make it much your own
For you deserve a life of joy
And richness to be honed

I say to you tomorrow
Will be the only day
That we can be together
And say we had today

Let's put this time behind us
And call this one for bliss
I love our new beginning
And I shall be here for this.

APPENDIX D

Benefits of Meditation

Meditation is the process by which you quiet your thoughts, the thoughts that go through your mind as you are in a waking state of consciousness. To begin a discipline of meditation only takes a few minutes of your time each day. My suggestion is that you meditate for ten minutes during each session, preferably three times each day.

This isn't always possible when beginning a meditation regimen. Sometimes life becomes so busy that meditation is the furthest thing from your mind. Try to make meditation the first thing on your agenda each day. As you awake, give yourself ten minutes to just *be*. If your mind is constantly wandering, obsessing or not staying focused, then take the first thing that you think about or see as you wake up. Latch onto that thought and, without obsessing on the object of the thought, begin to really focus on the actual thought. Watch what you think about that object without judgment. Do not analyze why your thought went in such direction. Just allow it to *be*.

The human mind is designed to analyze. That's its

intended purpose within the human condition. Without the ability to analyze, we wouldn't continue to exist. We analyze everything from what the red light means to financial matters at work; from relationships to car parts. The design of the human mind is very complex. We use it so much that we tend to forget we have these abilities.

Meditation will help you analyze because it gives the mind a break. When you sleep at night, it gives your physical body time to rest and rejuvenate, but your mind is still active. When you meditate, you are giving a period of time to your mind so that it can have its resting period. This is the time when you can shut off the world and truly tune in to your mind. We nourish our bodies with food and sleep, but when do we nourish our minds except through meditation and quiet time?

It's not so hard to designate quiet time. You already take time to cleanse your physical body. You shower or bathe. Why not take time to cleanse your mind each day?

Some people are more comfortable with mental energy. Their inclination is to be more mental, if you will. There are other people who are more physical or emotional. Meditation helps the physical and emotional processes as well. Great athletes often take time to visualize their games and the moves that they are going to make. They see themselves in their inner minds as being successful. You can do this, too. Meditation gives your mind the time to look at your success.

The mind has no judgment. However, we develop opinions and judgments based on many different factors. The mind settles when in meditation. If your thinking is scattered, during meditation it has time to sort through some of the scattered thoughts. If you're having trouble focusing on certain aspects of your daily life, meditation gives your mind an opportunity to experience the focusing process. Many people are not good at focusing. It is not their best attribute, but through the process of meditation, the mind can be disciplined to focus. That is its original purpose.

If you are too busy to give your mind an opportunity to settle into itself and just *be*, your body could become the victim of this neglect and constant stress. Activity without focus will take its toll on the body. The body needs the mind to function properly. Meditation gives the mind time within each twenty-four-hour period to nourish itself and gather itself. Three times a day, traditionally, the body is given food. We nourish the body three times per day, but when do we nourish the mind? When do we feed our thought process?

The average human brain uses less than ten percent of its capacity. What do we suppose the other ninety percent is there to do? We must develop our consciousness as a people. This is required of us by our higher intelligence. Almost everyone has had an enlightened experience; a moment in time when we tap into the higher intelligence. You have a creative thought about something that is very rudimentary. You say, "Oh, my, where did that thought come from? It solved my problem." Through the process of meditation on a regular basis you will have more enlightened ideas.

These ideas won't necessarily come to you during your meditation, but quieting the mind for a certain amount of time each day allows the mind to function more fluently all throughout the day. So these ideas may come to you at odd times, when you least expect them. If everyone in the population began to meditate regularly we would be able to tap into a group consciousness, which would elevate our level of thinking and thus accelerate what we can do on this planet. It would create cohesiveness, a group experience of the mind.

Many fine scientists, mathematicians, and spiritual intellects have attempted to bring meditation into our society. It hasn't worked well. The main reason for this is because we have been coerced into believing that we must work very hard and continuously for our daily bread. This keeps our bodies and our minds active and repeatedly thinking about working to make a living. It is true that we must work to live. But our work doesn't have to take us so far into activity that we have no time for the mind; no time for the thought processes of higher consciousness. That is the trick, you see.

Give yourself thirty minutes every day to tap into your higher consciousness. Do not judge what comes through in your meditation period. Allow whatever is there to be there. Should you experience some negative emotion in this meditation time, realize that all emotion is valid and it should be given a breath. Many people deny their true emotions and run from these sensations because they don't necessarily feel good.

Give your emotions time to breathe. If you do this in meditation, should you experience fear or anger, allow it to just be fear or anger in your body. Do not attach it to a thought. Just allow the fear, or the anger, or the sadness to be there with you at that time. Do not run from it. It will not hurt you if you give it a chance to breathe. During your meditation time the strong feelings have a voice, an opportunity to tell you *why* they are working for you. Allow the emotion to speak to you and tell you why it is with you.

Perhaps you have not properly grieved the death of a loved one, and hence your body is filled with sadness. In meditation time you can grieve: ten, twenty, or thirty minutes, or longer if you must, but you have that designated time to allow the emotion to breathe.

Perhaps you are angry with a friend or partner. During meditation you can be very angry and just sit with that anger. You can look at all sides of the anger. Perhaps the anger does not serve you well and you have been hurting others because of it and not recognizing the truth behind the anger. Meditation gives time to that anger and time for you to experience the truth about it. At the end of your meditation you can ask the anger to work more effectively for you. You can ask it to leave. You can ask your higher consciousness to help you work through this anger.

The same is true with fear. You will have a chance to look at what scares you. Many of our fear-based responses are not valid responses in this day and age. Fear does serve a purpose, so it is good to look at your fears and see which ones might be logical for your daily experience and which ones you can throw away. Meditation gives you time to handle emotion so that emotion does not rule your life.

Meditation also gives you the opportunity to connect with higher consciousness. So significant is the belief in guardian angels that there must be truth to this creed. Meditation gives you time to communicate with your guardians, whether you call them angels, or guides, or gurus. You have a master intelligence working within your own consciousness. Everything is comprised of energy. It is the same energy that makes up your tables and chairs and also your physical body. Indeed there are different chemicals, combinations of energies, and the DNA that makes you an individual. We all have the ability to use our higher consciousness.

Judeo-Christian scriptures tell us that humans ate the fruit from of the tree of knowledge. We have the ability as humans to ascertain the difference between good and evil, the difference between black and white, love and hate, mother and child. We have these innate abilities to discern, to know the difference. This is a gift, a blessing that humans have been given. We should take advantage of these offerings and give some back to the universal consciousness.

Every time a human being sits in meditation and is willing to receive the higher intelligence for just ten minutes, there is great celebration.

Every time you allow the mind to have a chance to speak to you, it is given validity. The first-grade child needs affirmation, needs to be told that he or she is doing good work in school; most adults realize that children need validation. Your mind is like a child needing validation. Your mind has worked for you all of this lifetime, be it twenty, thirty, forty, or more years, and (if you believe in reincarnation) for lifetimes. We need to give the mind opportunities to work for us. We are not robots. We have the ability to feel and tap into levels of consciousness that the animal kingdom cannot. We should appreciate these abilities and make use of them.

The mind is like a muscle in the body. If you do not use certain muscles they can atrophy and become a mass of useless material. The mind will do the same if we don't use it. Meditation gives the mind time to work properly. The mind stays active even when it's in a state of apathy or non-use. It will find something to do *somewhere*. What it is doing may be not at all be related to what is going on in your life, but it does not know that, since you don't give it time to just *be* with you as the receiver.

The more meditation you do, the more you will be able stay on top of your thoughts throughout the day. It will give you a chance to think before you act. So your actions will change. Your responses to people and events will change. You will become more serene and at peace with yourself and your experience.

The proper way to change anything is not through resistance and continual aggression, but through love and acceptance. Meditation will change your inner reality and therefore extend itself to your reactions and deeds toward others. The strongest of people have very disciplined minds and are mindful at all times. They might be involved in robotic activity, but they are mindful. They give the mind time to breathe.

Meditation can be fun. If you find yourself not being able to stay focused, then you might want to try a process of visualization and add some relaxing music in the background. There are many meditation processes by which you can give your mind a focus. Many religious traditions have processes of meditation.

Prayer is a process of meditation. Listening to music can be meditative. Whatever works for you is what works. With visualization you can create yourself. You might try putting affirmations with music on tape and listen to the tape regularly. Discover your best way of integrating: auditory, visual, kinesthetic, absolute silence, or music that soothes.

Create a safe place within your mind when you meditate. Perhaps a lovely outdoor setting will become your safe haven, or perhaps a place that you went to as a child and felt safe. Recreate it in your mind. Meditation is not an empty void. At times there may be nothing to which you can attach with your mind in meditation. Let the void experience work for you. Perhaps your mind is tired of thoughts and working and it needs a blank slate from which to work. Give it time to be completely empty if that is required.

The important thing is that you stay disciplined with your meditation. Do it on a regular basis, just like you might do a regimen of physical exercise. Also, give your mind time to exercise. Perhaps there is a way to combine the three: physical exercise, music and mental meditation.

People are individual in their preferences. A part of our blessed design is that each of us is unique while also being the same as each other. One person may enjoy a certain meditation discipline whereas another person may not receive any benefits from the same type of process. You must find what works for you, what you enjoy and what calls out to you every day.

Many people find that once they start meditating, they cannot stop. It becomes a craving, a healthy way for the body, mind and soul to connect. So they begin to crave meditation time. This is *good*. Give meditation a chance in your life. Doing it daily for three weeks should indicate to you the benefits of meditation, of knowing yourself, and of loving yourself.

APPENDIX E

Intuitive Hunches and Song

Please visit www.dreamtimepublishing.com/books.php for a downloadable version of this appendix.

Intuition comes to you as a sense that something is right or wrong, or just as a special knowledge about anything in life. Some people live strictly by this inner knowledge. They follow it in every moment. But other people are not familiar with the intuition and find themselves not in the flow quite often. To be "with" the flow, to operate in one's truest form, it helps to recognize those intuitive hunches that come as physical or emotional sensations in the body.

Equating these hunches with music will help the memory "remember" the next time you feel this way so that you can "know" that your intuition is speaking to you.

Every person will feel intuition in a different manner. Most people say that they "just know" when their intuition is instructing them. Many people learn lessons by not listening to their intuition and having to repeat certain dramas in their lives. You can save a lot of time and misery by beginning to pay attention to the clues that your intuition presents to you.

Intuition is a direct perception that something is right, bypassing logical thinking or reasoning. It comes in as a quick insight or very keen sense that something should be looked at or is happening. Intuition can be intercepted by fear, guilt, anger, or grief, so it's important to be aware of your feelings and keep them in check. Do not deny feelings, but make sure that you recognize deep-seated emotion so that it does not interfere with your truth.

Being in touch with intuitive hunches will help you develop clarity, and adding music to the mix will help you enjoy the process. These exercises will help you to become aware in the moment. Begin practicing living an intuitive life with music. It will be fun and tuneful, for sure!

Keep an intuitive music journal. For each hour of your waking day, write down one significant intuitive hunch that you had, which ones you acted on, and a song that reminds you of each hunch.

In other words, which actions did you take, or perceptions did you have, based on intuition that felt right and kept you "in flow?"

As a fun addendum, find a song that reminds you of each hunch you had during the day. For example, if you have a hunch about calling your friend Amanda, make the call and find that she is delighted to hear from you, then you may listen to and record the song *Amanda*.

HOUR 1 • Intuitive hunch:

Song related to hunch:

HOUR 2 • Intuitive hunch:

Song related to hunch:

HOUR 3 • Intuitive hunch:

Song related to hunch:

HOUR 4 • Intuitive hunch:

Song related to hunch:

HOUR 5 • Intuitive hunch:

Song related to hunch:

HOUR 6 • Intuitive hunch:

Song related to hunch:

HOUR 7 • Intuitive hunch:

Song related to hunch:

HOUR 8 • Intuitive hunch:

Song related to hunch:

HOUR 9 • Intuitive hunch:

Song related to hunch:

HOUR 10 • Intuitive hunch:

Song related to hunch:

HOUR 11 • Intuitive hunch:

Song related to hunch:

HOUR 12 • Intuitive hunch:

Song related to hunch:

Singing Visualization for Creativity

This exercise can most effectively be used in a group to promote cohesiveness and non-judgmental cooperation among participants.

Visualization: Play some very gentle familiar music in the background or through a headset or stereo. Sit quietly and relax. Close your eyes and begin to hum softly along with the music. Imagine that your voice is carried through the air; it gently fills the room or the area in which you are sitting. Do this without raising the volume of your voice.

Now begin to vocalize an *oooo* sound to the music, but very softly. Imagine your voice filling the space around you. See your voice in form as it fills the room. It has a very beautiful look and feel to it as you see it in your imagination. It can become anything you want it to become: an angel, a beautiful plant or crystal, a child, a new car or home, or even a picture of an upcoming action or performance in which you must participate . . . anything you want your voice to be in this moment, it is becoming.

Now change your vocalization to a soft *ahhh* sound,

singing along to the music. Fill the room with the *ahhh* sound. Imagine how the area around you changes. It becomes whatever you can envision.

Go back to a soft hum. Increase the volume just a bit and open your eyes. See the sound of your voice drifting off into the room. See the room filling with a beautiful light. Stop humming and just be silent for a few minutes. Notice any changes. Write down any significant insights you discovered in this process.

If you did this exercise with a group, discuss what you each discovered. To create a unified focus within a group, do this exercise again and visualize the desired outcome while singing the various sounds to the background music.

Benefits of Singing

1. Your singing voice can become anything you want it to become while you are visualizing.

2. Your voice can become a magnet to pull to you that which you want to create in your life.

3. Singing has the potential to make you feel well, energetic, and positive. It can be a healing force for all things in your life. Try out different vocalizations to see what sensations they create in your body.

4. Use the Ohm (vocalizing the Ohm in group or individually) to promote well-being and balance.

5. Singing can make you feel more confident in other areas of your life—teaching, public speaking, selling, customer

service—or to enhance your performance in other arts: dance, visual arts, etc. Building confidence in one area will always increase confidence in others.

6. Humming or singing in public places can increase the joviality of other people in the room. It shows that you are happy and has the tendency to rub off on other people.

Write your public singing experiences here:

Glossary

A cappella: singing without instrumental accompaniment

Alto: low female voice; contralto, second highest part in choral or part music

Bass: low male voice; lowest part in choral or part music

Cantor: an official whose duty it is to lead the liturgical or singing/chanting parts of prayer in churches or synagogues

Falsetto: an unnatural or unusually high-pitched voice, in a man or an alto voice

Larynx: a muscular and cartilaginous structure lined with mucus membrane at the upper part of the trachea, in which the vocal cords are located

Octave: eight notes in succession comprise one octave

Perfect (absolute) pitch: the ability to sing or recognize the pitch of a tone by ear

Pharynx: the tube with its surrounding membrane and muscles that connects the mouth and nasal passages to the esophagus

Pitch: key or keynote of a melody

Rhythm: the pattern of regular or irregular pulses in music caused by the occurrence of strong and weak melodic and harmonic beats

Rounds: a short rhythmical canon at the unison, in which several individual voices or groups of voices enter in at equally spaced intervals

Soprano: high female voice; highest part in choral or part music

Tenor: high male voice; third highest part in choral or part music

Timbre: the characteristic quality of sound produced by a particular instrument or voice (tonal color)

Vibrato: a pulsating effect, produced in singing by a rapid change of pitch

Visualization: to recall or form mental images

Vocal Cords: either of two pairs of folds of mucus membrane projecting into the cavity of the larynx

Vocal Folds (true vocal cords): the lower pair of vocal cords, the edges of which can be made to tense and relax by the passage of air from the lungs, thus producing vocal sounds.

Resources

Books

Cirlot, J. E, A *Dictionary of Symbols*, New York, NY: Philosophical Library, 1971. Now out of print, I use this book often to find historically correct symbology meanings from many traditions. An excellent resource. It has been revised in a 2002 paperback edition with same title/author, published by Dover Publications.

Love, Roger and Frazier, Donna, *Set Your Voice Free: How to Get the Singing or Speaking Voice You Want:* Little, Brown and Company, 1999 and 2003. A fun way to learn to love your voice while practicing to make it perfect.

Phillips, Pamelia S., *Singing for Dummies*, New York, NY: Wiley Publishing, Inc., 2003. An overview of everything one might want to know about the basics of learning to sing. She offers many techniques, references and information on singing for fun and even prepare professionally.

Websites

Please note that website addresses often disappear or change. The Internet is always in flux, but these are just a few of the sites that I've enjoyed.

America's Got Talent (nbc.com/Americas_Got_Talent). All the latest on the AGT television show and how to apply for an audition.

Chorus America (chorusamerica.org/index.cfm). Learn almost everything you want to know about choral singing from the benefits of it, where to find a choir locally, conductor's information, and much more.

Country Music Television (cmt.com). Get all the up to date news on your favorite country artists and music.

John Denver (johndenver.com/index.htm). John Denver's official site.

Dog and Pony Sound Singing Tips (dogandponysound.com/sing_tip_singmag0.htm). Lots of good, short articles from what seems to be some pretty professional folk.

The Internet Sacred Text Archive, article "The Pythagorean Theory of Music and Color," (sacred-texts.com/eso/sta/sta19.htm). This site is rich with ancient and current information, anything relative to metaphysics, religions and sacred mysteries.

KSolo, Everybody Sings (ksolo.com). Karaoke live! Record your favorite karaoke on the computer, send it out, join competitions, find karaoke music . . . and more.

Amanda McBroom, The History of The Rose (amcbroom.com/rose.html). An interesting story of how *The Rose* came to be written and performed as theme song for the movie of same title. Go to Amanda McBroom's homepage for information on her tour schedule and other songs she has written.

Index

About the Author

Jules Kennedy has been teaching, counseling, and writing in the areas of metaphysics and spirituality since 1984. She holds a B.S. in Human Development and Counseling, with additional coursework in religion and women's studies. She has pursued a diverse career path in social work, volunteer administration, counseling, and psychic advising. She has clientele and students worldwide. She currently does psychic advising and business consulting by phone and email, and lectures at various events.

Jules has traveled with her husband to places throughout the United States. The couple relocates whenever they feel the call within, but currently lives in Indiana. She is also the author of *Dimensional Ascension: Multi-Dimensional Living for Light Workers* and can be reached through her website at JulesKennedy.com.

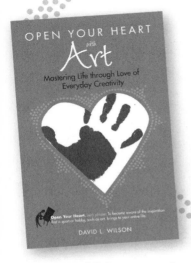

Contests, new titles, events, news, discussion and feedback. Sign up for your latest chance to win, and find out about upcoming books at **www.dreamtimepublishing.com**

OUR COMMUNITY

DreamTime Publishing supports the community by participating regularly in worthwhile fundraising and charitable efforts. Let us know what's important to you, and sign up at **www.dreamtimepublishing.com** to find out what's happening near you.

ONLINE BOOK CLUB AND MORE!

Come by and share in a discussion of the latest books from top authors and leave your feedback on DreamTime Publishing's titles and for our authors. Sign up at **www.dreamtimepublishing.com** to get the latest information.

WHAT'S GOING ON?

Check out our online calendar for events and appearances by DreamTime authors. Sign up at **www.dreamtimepublishing.com** to make sure you don't miss anything!